AF701754

Starting Over

Starting Over

How to Recharge Your Life-Style and Career— With Firsthand Accounts of the New Pioneers Who've Done It

ALLAN A. SWENSON

A & W Publishers, Inc.
New York

Copyright © 1978 by Allan A. Swenson

All rights reserved. No part of this work may be reproduced or transmitted in any form or by any means, electronic or mechanical, including photocopying, recording, or any information storage and retrieval system, without the permission in writing from the publishers.

Published by
A & W Publishers, Inc.
95 Madison Avenue
New York, New York 10016

Library of Congress Catalog Card Number: 78-53416

ISBN: 0-89479-018-8

Designed by Helen Roberts

Printed in the United States of America

Contents

Starting Over—An Introduction

You may, surprisingly enough, see yourself reflected in this book. It may even encourage you to change your course and pursue your own destiny on a far different path and in a different direction from that you now follow. That choice is yours.

This book is about new pioneers: the seekers of happier lives, the makers and shakers of a better world today and tomorrow. Some have felt like expatriates or refugees in America, fleeing from jobs, lives (sometimes even wives and husbands), and situations they dislike and reject. But they are the new blood of the country, the new spirit of independence, self-sufficiency, and vitality, that is ascending again.

The new pioneers are many different people: men and women young and old, married and single, divorced and left alone by death, who have forged and continue to forge a new life for themselves. In a very real sense, they've started their lives over. These people are the renewed strength of America, reborn spirits echoing the heritage that made America the boldest, strongest, most resilient and the best nation the world has seen.

They are what you can be, perhaps should be, when and where you desire. That decision is yours. There are a few places on this planet where people can still make a choice and see it through.

This book is about those who have broken away from well-established lives, careers, and communities and have transplanted themselves. Some have been content, some have succeeded monetarily as well. Others have learned that starting over isn't always peaches and cream. Old jobs have looked glamorous in retrospect, when winter winds howled and fuel bills went unpaid. Some have not once looked back and have seldom winced as they adjusted to their new life-styles.

This book, revised several years from now, could be about you, alone or with your family. That decision, if you believe in yourself and the opportunities abounding around you, is yours to make on your own and in concert with the ones you love. Those in this book have made their choice. They have moved from city and suburb, as more are moving across America today. They are different in some ways from the original pioneers in Conestoga wagons, but similar in many other ways. New pioneers may drive vans or pickup trucks instead. They aren't necessarily seeking gold and riches. Tens of thousands of people are on the move, pulling up long-established roots to transplant themselves and their families into a new world of their own design.

They are, in fact, more like the old pioneers who opened up America's frontiers than many of them realize. They long for openness, not just in space, but in their dealings with other people. They have a give-and-take attitude that lets them relax and be themselves as human beings. They have a spirit of independence, a frankness and honesty with each other and their fellow man that make them close kin to pioneers of years ago. This reviving pioneer spirit is indeed alive and well and growing stronger each week and month across our land.

You may be a new pioneer at heart; or maybe the man in the next office, the woman working next to you, the family living down the street, are new pioneers. Some feel themselves caught in a mainstream of life they don't understand or enjoy. Some feel they are living and biding their time while they plot and plan their own personal escape to a better life.

Across America, people like you are thinking their secret thoughts about the lives they lead, their jobs, their families, their hopes, fears, and desires. There are millions of people like you who want something more fulfilling out of their time on earth than what they now have. Many find their present jobs dull, commuting a bore, crowded cities beyond bearing. They experience their career as unchallenging, their community as disoriented. Millions have fled the cities already, only to find suburbia too starkly structured and status-conscious.

Thousands upon thousands of people are leaving the suburbs they once called home. They are leaving cities, too, giving up "good" jobs, modern homes, and the financial strains of big mortgages. This phenomenon is not a tidal wave, nor is it a flood of fleeing humanity; not yet. Rather, it is a steady stream of people like you that is growing larger with each passing year.

If you have the urge to look around for greener pastures . . . you're not alone. If you aren't satisfied with your job or career . . . others feel as you do. If you believe you can pick yourself up and become what you really think you could and should be, others have done that, too. There's room for you among the new pioneers.

Among the new pioneers are lawyers and mechanics, teachers and salespeople, businessmen and clerks. There are top executives running local country stores, ex-bankers making potato chips, housewives who have become artists and book illustrators; a woman who is warmed by her wood stove sales success, an accountant turned artist and dump lecturer.

Like the youths of the sixties and, more recently, those who rebelled against what to them was an overly materialistic, structured society, these individuals and families are searching for something different, more meaningful, more personally satisfying. Unlike youthful dropouts, however, these new pioneers range in age from the late twenties to over fifty. They still take themselves seriously and have a deep sense of responsibility to themselves and others.

Some work longer, harder, and more happily for themselves; others have not sought financial rewards. Most put primary emphasis on peace of mind, contentment, and a more natural pace of life. They seem in tune with nature.

You too may feel the itch and urge that motivates the new pioneers. You may have had, from time to time, a vague restlessness, an uneasy feeling that all isn't quite right and as it should be with your life. If so, you are in good company. The feeling that a person can and should take control of his or her personal destiny seems to be shared by all the new pioneers.

From these people—from their ideas, goals, hopes, fears, false starts, and successes—you can find a guide to the trail of the new pioneers. The trail may curve and wind and twist back on itself at times. But it has been clearly marked by the actions of those who have traveled it and are still moving toward the new destination that they seek. You can benefit from their experience in many ways. Their guideposts and blazemarks can help you plan your own transplanting and rerooting. You can learn how to search for a new career, hometown, community, and life-style, whether in Florida, Maine, or Colorado, from coastal town to rural village or mountain retreat.

You'll discover some of the vital signs to be learned at a local coffee counter, barber or beauty shop, or supermarket. From new pioneers you will learn key questions to ask bankers, boards of education, employment offices, local business people, and the person on the street, as you begin your own new pioneering.

Other chapters will expand on the search pattern you can follow. You'll find tips on reading between the lines of what realtors say and what they really mean, as well as on how to learn whether the communities you explore will meet your desires for a new home.

Other chapters, basic to rerooting, will help you settle in comfortably, whether you wish to blend into the surroundings or take an active part in your new community affairs. From the chapters about new pioneer themselves, you'll realize how easy it can be to become "downward mobile" (as one man describes his view of what he had done). Actually, many people starting over have left what are conventionally and politely accepted as "good" jobs, "nice" homes, and "respectable" communities, to settle for far less than their former neighbors and coworkers consider the "essentials" of living.

As one new pioneer vividly expressed it, standing at the shore of his lakeside cottage at sunset:

"Yes, I've given up many essentials, things I once thought were vitally important. I've given up large monthly mortgage payments on a house in a fashionable neighborhood, car payments on two new, prestigious cars, high taxes so I could live in a respectable suburb, big liquor bills so I could be invited to the proper cocktail parties. I've given up a lot and now I can stop and really see a sunset."

You'll find kindred souls in this book, and you may find some who astound or puzzle you. Some you may learn to love and others perhaps envy. There are patterns you can elect to follow if you choose to take the path they took.

There have been decisions made by these people as they started over—good and bad decisions. Assessing both, you can judge which way you wish to move. From their examples and from the lessons learned by these who moved on before, you may decide to plod, walk, or run to the new goals you set for yourself.

If you find a judgment here or there, please pardon them. They reflect the attitudes of the people who participated in the preparation of this book. You will find the thoughts, right or wrong, good or bad, of the *real people* whose experiences comprise this book. You can bet they are real.

I've spent uncounted hours talking, visiting, working, commiserating, and celebrating with these people. They are truly the new pioneers, and from their lives you too can discover more new frontiers and horizons than you ever thought possible.

This book is dedicated to those people and the thousands like them from all walks of life who now enjoy different, happier lives.

I salute the new pioneers with gratitude. They may not yet be a flood tide sweeping all before it. But they are, without a doubt, a sign of things to come. They are like the ripples of a pebble flung into a quiet pond. The ripples they create are far-reaching, causing currents that carry across a nation.

This book is dedicated to the new pioneers, whoever and wherever you are, and whatever you wish to be.

Allan A. Swenson
Windrows Farm
Kennebunk, Maine

Starting Over

1/The Itch Begins

Like Daniel Boone, many people feel the world is closing in around them. Boone responded by packing up and moving across mountains when just one neighbor built a cabin in the same valley he occupied. Many among today's masses of humanity may have that same feeling of restlessness, but there are precious few virgin valleys left.

Besides, the constraints of a job, the need to earn an income to satisfy the need for creature comforts—these tend to keep most people where they are. Escape from the pressures of the cities was possible, at least, and that served a useful purpose for soon-to-be pioneers. Just across the city line lay suburbia with its trees, homes, and gardens, with country clubs and all the greener grass that many saw as their more pleasant portion of the planet Earth. Flight from the cities has been steady for several decades. For millions, suburbia was the new frontier they sought.

The fact is, many Americans have become so accustomed to the proliferation of housing developments, to strip cities and the highways that connect them, that they seem oblivious to the sprawl that has been engulfing the open areas to which they fled. Much of this continuous outward flow and flight from cities seems to have gone unnoticed by those who hurried to that greener pasture just across the city line. What was once the Garden State of New Jersey today looks more like a parking lot for New York and Philadelphia. Other areas, too, look much the same.

During the past two decades, paving of America was begun in earnest. As more people fled the confines of the city, they brought with them their conditioned reflexes: the needs for street lights, sidewalks, the instant conveniences of shopping malls, twenty-four-hour service centers—the essentials they required in the world they fled. The paving of America continued outward. Woods were cut, streams diverted, floodplains built upon as strip city developments arose. Many people became large frogs in smaller ponds.

A frog, you may have heard, is often slow to respond to slow change. It can be placed in a pot of water and swim about contentedly. If the water is heated slowly, the frog will still swim around until it is fully cooked. People tend to be like frogs at times. If life changes gradually enough around them, if their bellies are full and they have their creature comforts, they too will mill about in unwitting contentment.

Beneath the surface, however, there seems to be a vague uneasiness that many people are feeling more today than in past decades. You may know the feeling yourself. It may begin as an itch, perhaps an irritation or two. Vacations aren't as restful as they once were. You may feel it takes longer to settle back in harness after a few weeks of vacation from your job. Little things that once were overlooked assume more importance: Your boss is grumpier, your commute to work less tolerable; the neighbors may seem nosier and government less receptive to your wishes. There's a mood that seems to say, "If only someone would do something, things would be better." If you have felt something like this, you're not alone.

The pioneering spirit of Daniel Boone stirs deep within many of us today, and it is growing stronger every year. Today, even in the soothing green environment of the suburbs, there is a restlessness. At times it rises to a level where corporation psychologists, industrial relations specialists, and sociologists can examine it more closely. To many of these observers, the phenomonon of the new pioneer is an enigma. The underlying reason for the desire to move on is not easily uncovered.

The Gallup survey has focused on the increased mobility of Americans in recent years. The highly regarded public opinion organization has found that this mobility seems likely to continue into the foreseeable future. The firm's recent surveys reveal that one person in five—nearly 20 percent—says they do not expect to be living in their present community five years from now. Another 7 percent is uncertain.

Many observers of the current American mobility phenomonon attribute it to the breakdown of the family unit. Others see the restlessness as reflecting lack of satisfaction and challenge in the jobs that people do for their living.

The most mobile group among Americans are young adults. That's understandable; their roots have not been set down too deeply. One third of them say that they expect to live in a different community within the next five years. But restlessness is not confined to the younger generation. Older individuals, couples with grown children also are looking to move somewhere, somehow, sometime soon. Their reasons often are not clear to themselves. But move they will.

Important in their thinking—as verified by several surveys establishing the mobility phenomonon—is one underlying motivation: a desire to escape big-city living. Other studies, by companies and research firms hired to analyze the increasing turn toward mobility of corporate employees, suggest other answers. These include disenchantment with career goals, boredom with the job, lack of challenge, or excess pressure to conform. The answers offered by the learned often are conflicting.

One thing is certain. People, as they analyze their career goals and personal desires, are becoming more aware that they are really restless. One phrase emerges most often. It is simply, "There must be something better."

Whether companies or giant corporations can stem the wave of mobility is debatable. Executives, once eager to scramble up the corporate ladder to assume exalted positions in the hierarchy, have become markedly less so. Many firms are discovering that offers of deserved promotions are being turned down by otherwise loyal employees.

"We even have had employees threaten to quit or join the competition if we forced them to take a promotion, or move to corporate headquarters into higher management positions," one somewhat astonished corporate executive says. "In the last year alone, we had several really excellent people leave for no good reason. They just seemed to be uninterested in getting ahead any further." His experience is not uncommon.

And yet, these same people may turn around tomorrow to switch jobs, join other firms, and move again. Some claim they have found an area of the country that they like and want to try another job for a time. Others can place their fingers on their own pulse, but can't explain what it is they feel or why they can't remain in one place or job too long. Social scientists and corporate committees alike have theories and even logical-sounding explanations for the restlessness that seems to pervade society and their employee ranks today.

There is another explanation.

The migration to the cities for the best jobs, the big

paycheck, the climb to success, left people hungry. Their success may have fed them well in other ways, but it left an inner emptiness. As corporations, unions, and governments grew larger, they became less responsive to the individual's personal sense of accomplishment. Men and women were fit into neatly designed, specialized functions. Whether they screwed a nut into place on an assembly line or closed a new sales contract, they were only cogs in the gigantic wheel of progress. It rolled merrily along with or without them.

Millions in the work force, whether at a store, factory, office job or in the home, felt unfulfilled. They seldom saw the end results of their own efforts. Instead of being valued as people, they were judged by what they seemed to be, what they had, what they could afford to display; a home, a car, a different-colored office chair or the first snowmobile on the block.

"Money isn't all that bad," a new pioneer explained. "It was the way you were judged based on the money you spent and what it bought that bugged me." Somewhere along the way, the spirit of the game had been lost. Winning at all costs was important, not the fun of winning. The system had become paramount, rather than the people who made the system work.

Other new pioneers reflected on why they too cut the cord that tied them to their previous life and career.

"I found myself like Pavlov's dogs, salivating on cue but for what really seemed like the wrong cues," a former banker pointed out.

"Sometimes I had to ask myself on Friday, what it was that I had really done that whole week," an accountant said. "On Monday, it was the same thing again, check the ledger, fill out the forms, post the bloody books," he paints watercolors now.

"It didn't really seem important to have all the jeeps and trucks lined up just so, every bumper in a line you could check with a surveyor's scope," a former soldier said, thinking back to the hours lining up the motor pool for Saturday inspection.

"I realized that there just couldn't be that many wives who didn't understand their husbands, which is what I heard ten times a week from the guys who gave me dictation," a secretary added.

"Nobody could read the Brooks Brothers label because it was stitched on the inside of my suit coat," a former ad man remembers.

"I really couldn't get excited about vacuuming another hundred miles of rugs," one housewife says.

"When we paid a vault tax, I began adding up the taxes we paid in the city. The city tax people justified a vault tax because we had the garbage elevator in the basement that came up through the sidewalk through a vault and interrupted pedestrian traffic once a day," a former restaurateur recalls.

"Beefeater gin, Chivas Regal—having the right brand names to impress your cocktail party guests finally got to me," a former sales executive noted.

Little things, the last straws, perhaps; but a chance remark, a brief encounter, a minor episode are the landmarks that many of the new pioneers recall as they look back at their decisions.

"It wasn't a momentous decision like moving to the Yukon or packing up the family in a wagon train to fight Indians all the way to California, nothing like that at all," one says grudgingly. "I wouldn't have had the guts to do that. All we really did was turn ourselves around and head off in another direction. It seemed like the thing to do, give up the rat race for a slower pace that would let us enjoy each other more and have more time to do the things we really wanted . . . even lie in the backyard and look at the stars, or watch the kids catch lightning bugs."

The new pioneers are kindred spirits whether they realize it or not, although most have not met each other and probably never will. They share the same desire to emerge from the confines of status-conscious towns or structured corporate life. They share the need to be on their own, to win or lose, but at their own hands. All of them share an openness and a feeling that they can and should control their own destinations in order to take advantage of what life has to offer.

Not surprisingly, they share an appreciation of nature. Some believe that their decision was based in part on a feeling that the world was too much chrome and plastic. Others point to greater concern with preserving the environment. As one put it, ". . . there's still something worth preserving left. I wanted to get back to basics: raise animals, watch flowers grow, walk on a beach in winter when I'm there all alone, just me and the wind and the waves."

Another, looking back with no regrets, admits, "We may have traded shares in America's largest corporations on the floor of the Big Board at the Stock Exchange, but now I'm trading livestock: two sows for a pony that my daughter can ride down by the brook in our meadow. That's a better trade."

Some wanted more challenging jobs. As they looked ahead, they saw nothing but more boredom heaped in hills before them. Factory worker or secretary, salesperson or business executive, the road ahead looked unrewarding. Even those who were acknowledged to be skilled in their positions, destined for promotions they deserved, had second thoughts about the life they led. To them, the path ahead didn't seem to lead in the direction they wanted to go.

Some, of course, wanted more time for themselves. The daily commute, fighting traffic to and from work, the lines in cafeterias or even at the bar on the way home, made them rethink their real desires.

"It's the same old hassle every day," one young executive remarked. "Get up, catch the train, walk across town, get in the elevator, walk down the hall, answer the phones, fill out the orders. Then the same thing all the way home. I wasted hours every day."

Another looked back at what he now says were twenty

wasted years with the same people around the coffee cart, the same gripes, the same office, the same desk. He was bored most of the time.

A one-time business executive slowly realized he was part of a pecking order in his work and his town. "Every cocktail party we attended, someone talked about a new promotion. They always wanted to know what level you were on so they could compare the level they were on, or their husband or cousin or someone down the street. It's become a pecking order every day.

"You would hear it in the car pool, at the tennis club, around the backyard swimming pool. There was always someone who wanted to know what you did, where you were in your company, so they could compare your rise up that glorious ladder of success with their own. And people still do it in my old home town.

"Are you a manager, a supervisor, a coordinator or what? They seem to want to put you in a nice neat slot each time you meet," he recalls with just the trace of a shudder. "God help you if you lose your job, you drop to zip-points on the pecking order scale."

One rising young executive recalls with horror the day he lost his job.

"My world had ended. I was a total washout, a failure at thirty-two. That wasn't my view at first, but I got the message in the first week I was out of work. I climbed aboard the train each day with all the friends I met commuting. We might read our paper, a trade magazine, play cards, or just talk. My wife played tennis, bridge, went shopping with their wives. I was caught in a merger. The company that took over already had enough district managers. Some had to go and I was one," he explained.

"Losing a good job is bad enough on your ego. Having to pay the monthly mortgage payments, the car installments, the furniture too, that scares you. I knew I could get another job but when you're on the beach, you need every contact you can get, every friend you have, but did they disappear

"People avoided me on the train. A few even moved to other cars. I felt like I had something contagious. When the word got out I was on the beach, the invitation to cocktail parties dribbled down to nothing. Invitations to my wife to play bridge or tennis evaporated. We were treated as though we were tainted."

One salesman kept a diary through his jobless weeks as he filled out applications, rewrote résumés, and knocked on doors.

"I have a 'feces roster' on the wall in my den at home, neatly framed. It includes all the names of my so-called friends.

"Guys I knew for years were on the phone long distance or in meetings when I called them. A few times they might have been, but every day I called to ask about a job?" he asks. "Secretaries I had known functioned perfectly too," he recalls. "They screened all calls efficiently, as though they thought I had a social disease."

Among new pioneers, a surprising number had been confronted with a loss of faith in friends who could have helped when times were tough, but didn't.

Others had no such experience. They were headed higher every year, and their financial rewards were varied. Promotions, bonuses, fringe benefits kept bills paid and left money for the frills of life. Among those who turned into new pioneers, a crosscurrent was the feeling of disenchantment with their steady climb to accepted goals of business success.

For some, the realization hit hard suddenly.

"I was sitting in my motel room in Kansas City," one recalls. "The convention was rolling along nice and smooth. Everything was clicking into place. I could see we would exceed our quotas. That meant money in the bank and probably the next promotion. In a way I felt elated. It all seemed so easy.

"The last thing I had to do was interview one of our area representatives for his promotion. He had everything going for him. He was well liked, he did his job better than anyone else at his level, he had an attractive wife and nice kids. We talked for about two hours. I asked all the questions on the company form. And I probed his likes and dislikes, his own personal goals. I asked the big question, where he saw himself ten years down the line. His answer wasn't anything that would startle you. He said he wanted more time to go fishing.

"After the interview was over, a few drinks tucked away at the end of another long day, I tried to remember when I had last been fishing.

"It had been almost three years back," the ex-sales manager adds. So he interviewed himself on an extra corporate questionnaire he carried. He also thumbed back through his executive pocket planner and counted the days spent in airline terminals, on planes, in motels, weekends away from home.

His new pioneer itch began that night. He scratched it hard all next day on the plane home. Two months later he was owner of a general store in the White Mountains of New Hampshire.

For some, the decision builds up slowly.

"Every time I turned in sales that made my assigned quota, the sales manager raised it. Twice he cut my territory so I had to hustle harder to make the quota," a traveling salesman explains.

"That wasn't too bad, really. The more I sold the more money I made. The company made money and I got my piece of the action, my commissions," he recalls.

"But I was away from home more, my daughter and son saw me on weekends only, and my wife kidded me about being Uncle Daddy, in front of the kids. It took me four years to make the move. Now I can go to their play or baseball game or take a day off for a picnic. I set my own quotas for work. Some days I'll put in eighteen hours too."

As he and his family backpack over another crest in the hills near their new home, they look back into the small valley. It is far removed from the world they swirled in before.

"It has a post office and that's all we need to run our mail order business from our own kitchen table and garage. We've settled down differently. We pay our bills and go to church again. It's a more peaceful life."

One question commonly asked by new pioneers dates back to a time they prefer to forget. It's a simple enough question: "What the hell am I doing here."

Oscar Adolph was an advertising man. He relished creating campaigns that could motivate millions to try new products and buy them again and again. The pressures were enormous—thinking up new ways to sell shampoo, dog food, cereal, or whatever other product needed a creative push at the time. The pay was higher than he could make in most any other field. He was admittedly overpaid, but he rationalized, "You are paid for the pressure they put you through in the ad game."

He had thought wistfully at times of vacations he would like to take. But crisis followed crisis—a TV commercial had to be shot, a campaign revised, copy lines changed to suit some client's quirk. Vacations could be postponed, client demands could not.

"I was heading for my office on Madison Avenue in the Big Apple one morning when I realized the leaves had turned brown on the trees. It dawned on me that I hadn't noticed they were changing color. That did it for me," he believes.

Restlessness, a wanderlust, a vague discontent—all these feelings at one time or another washed across the minds of the new pioneers. You may have experienced some of them yourself, and thought: out there somewhere there is a better way to go.

If so, it may be worthwhile to sit quietly in a corner today or first thing tomorrow morning. Let your mind flow backward to the things you've done, what you have accomplished, where you have been. Look at now, who you are, what you are doing presently. Take a hard look far ahead. Project yourself years ahead to the things you foresee for yourself, your family if you have one, or the ones you love and respect and want to share that future. It's not really hard to do. It may take time. It may take talk with those you trust, your family and your friends.

Some may not share your pioneering spirit. Others most likely will. If you take the time today or first thing in the morning to look ahead, there are things to be done to reach the new goals you are setting for yourself.

The blazes along the routes taken by the new pioneers can be especially valuable, for these people have rerooted themselves successfully. Their stories follow.

2/Planning Your Move

The urge to become a new pioneer is like a weed seed. It takes root quietly in the stillness of the night. The covering of the concept begins to open, revealing the central core of the new pioneering spirit and life that is within. New cells form, then a stalk, some leaves. Weeds are irrepressible. So is the new pioneering spirit.

You'll recognize the symptoms sure enough. You'll probe your reasons, assay your goals, perhaps meditate through what seems like endless hours of anguish in search of the right decision for your future.

For some, the ultimate decision has been described as much like the lifting of a giant hand that held them immobile. For others, there was a dawning new day, a sudden awakening to the realization that things could be changed. Still others have told of feeling reborn when they finally met themselves and made peace with themselves in a decision to walk new paths. The first obstacle was hurdled; the basic decision made; the quest begun.

The next step among the new pioneers is easier. It encompasses the more traditional decision-making process, developed in most of us from childhood through the long years of school. Some, it's true, simply yanked up roots and headed off to what they knew had to be that "better life." Of these, the more precipitous, some have regretted their hastiness. The vast majority pooled their creative powers with their friends, family, loved ones. They assessed their talents and abilities. They became pragmatic in their thinking.

Some readily admit they were fearful that their decision might end in failure if they made the wrong moves. Many confessed, too, that the thing they feared most was personal embarrassment and the mocking laughter of former friends and associates should they fall flat on their faces.

"One thing that haunted me the most," a former business executive reported, "was that after all my seeming success in the corporate world, I would fall apart on my own without the help of dozens of staff people to handle the many details of daily business operations. Translated, that means, 'Could I make it on my own?' " he adds.

Another, a specialist in the art of communications and persuasion, fretted even more.

"Envy is a big factor among people you assume were friends and allies," he explains. "They begrudge you your success and seem secretly to want to have their chance to laugh as you fall flat. That unfortunately is human nature. Many who won't take the risks, still want to see you fall back to their level of mediocrity. And that's what really scared me, that they would have their chance to laugh at me behind my back if I failed in my own business."

Most new pioneers had similar misgivings as they began walking the new path they had elected to travel. In a corporation there are *shared* risks, *group* discussion, *group* decisions. As one person put it, "Corporate meetings are verbal incest." Those who play the corporate game become well skilled not only in passing the buck but also in putting the responsibility for bad decisions on other people's backs. If a committee reaches a decision, and it goes sour, top management finds it difficult to place the blame on any one individual.

New pioneers, almost to a person, agreed that having to assume all the responsibilities for their decisions was one of the chief causes of their periodic misgivings. Yet few turned back.

Several voiced the prevalent attitude:

"We wanted challenge and personal freedom. To get that, you must take risks and make decisions on your own. And when you do, surprisingly enough, the challenge encourages you to move ahead. Challenge is stimulating, it makes you think and sweat."

"Fact is, every problem, every decision, made me realize I was better than I thought I was," a former banker says.

The actual uprooting and transition process varied among the new pioneers. Some picked up and fled with little thought until they landed in a desired new hometown. Others shopped for a small business, building their new life from that point. Still others, and actually most, more methodically developed a hard-nosed, logical, even cold-blooded analysis of how best to make their move.

One example may serve as a guide to their methodical shopping process for a new life, hometown, and life-style. In addition, it constitutes a composite of various people's modus operandi in their pioneering moves and during the critical transition period.

"We had had it with the overcrowding, social elbowing, artificially rushing pace, and cocktail party syndrome when our small town turned into a transient suburban bedroom city," Oscar Adolph points out. "We had become accustomed to an artificially inflated standard of living based on the high salary I made. I figured that the move out and away had better be planned carefully or I might be back on Madison Avenue, tail tucked between my legs, licking my wounds and pleading for work.

"I haunted coffee counters and barber shops. My wife visited beauty parlors. She had more hairdos in more styles in more places in a few months than she had in a year at home.

"I walked supermarket aisles with her too, pushing the cart. We asked people about food prices, got talking about the school system to find out what the principal or superintendent won't really tell you. There's a wealth of information available about any given area if you know how to dig it out."

Across America, coffee shops are favored gathering places for a wide cross section of people in their hometown. They are an ideal fact-finding resource center. Granted, some information is colored with local exaggeration and folklore. But the facts are there for you to weed out. Supermarkets also are gathering spots for millions of people. Wheeling carts down aisles, many people are eager to be friendly, provide shopping information for new neighbors, and pass along juicy bits of local gossip.

Barber and beauty shops also are fountains of information; they have had that tradition from our earliest days. You can pick up many pointers while sitting in a barber's chair, especially when you innocently ask questions about the area.

Realtors obviously are in business to provide information about homes, land, and conditions in their locality. Some are more eager to sell the property than to provide salient comments about the particular home or area. With probing questions you can ferret out the facts you need to know. By shopping with several realtors, you can compare notes from different points of view.

Don't overlook school board members if you have youngsters who will attend local schools. Members usually can be more forthright than the established working administration who parrot the official line. To make your transition planning and movement easier, perhaps a step-by-step guide, culled from many new pioneers, will be helpful. It's based on logical progessions which you might follow yourself. It includes often-overlooked sources of background information as well as ways the new pioneers have dug out the true facts about areas, homes, property, businesses, and the people among whom they put down their new roots.

Look far ahead into your desired future. That's the first key to picking a place on the planet where you can devote your time and energies to perfecting your new life-style. Think in terms of what it is you really want to do and be. If you like warm weather and outdoor living year round, look south, of course. As you do, remember that many others have fled harsh northern winters before you. They've flocked to Florida, Arizona, New Mexico, Southern California. That migration has been steady for a decade.

The Southwest has attracted tens of thousands of eastern Americans as factories, businesses, and consequently job opportunities have risen there. If you don't fancy roosting in a housing development side-by-side with transplanted suburbanites, cross such major areas as Tucson and Phoenix off your list. Orlando, Ft. Lauderdale, Sarasota in Florida may offer year-round outdoor living fun, but these too now sprawl for miles. Most new pioneers have chosen smaller towns to avoid life-styles like those they are attempting to leave behind.

Climate may or may not be a factor in your personal plans. Some new pioneers long for the privacy of a desert or the north woods. That desire for solitude is not what you may at first suspect; escape from other people. Rather, it is an underlying wish to move in smaller, less frantic circles where people tend to live and let live, rather than pass judgment on their neighbor's way of life.

You may be mountain minded or attracted to the

beauty of water, be it lake or bay, stream or ocean. If you seek to explore new horizons in harmony with natural surroundings, that of course will condition your choice of locality. Several factors will enter this phase of your planning.

For many new pioneers, finding a spot involves something of a pilgrimage. The dreams they, and perhaps you, have of 100 acres (more or less), open space, land, trees, a view of lake, river, or stream, can be real. Thousands upon thousands of pioneer spirits already have made their move. Many others are in process now.

One of the funniest stories told at real estate meetings in various towns, with modifications based on the circumstances, is the story of the young couple looking for their place in the country.

"They came into our office with a budget of $20,000, wanted a nice old farm with a rambling house, some buildings and about fifty acres or so of land, with maybe a nice stream running through the pasture. The barns had to be in good shape so they could work on their crafts and hobbies they were going to make into a business," old Hiram Stanhope chuckles. In reply to his story, ten other realtors have their own version from their personal experience. "We just suggest they get back in their car and head north. Maybe something nearer the Arctic Circle would be in their price range," Hiram chuckles again.

As you set out on your home-finding rounds, be realistic. The land you saw ten or fifteen years ago was low in price. So were the houses. Times have changed. The early birds moved first, as usual, and staked their claims years back.

Don't panic. There is room for you to reroot too. But you must realize that, although tales of land prices $50 to $150 per acre may be true enough, you'll be hard pressed to find those parcels of the planet Earth. Today supply and demand have caught up with dreams. Natives aren't restless; they just want their share of the selling price and a nice profit too, thank you.

The rule of thumb is, of course, the closer to towns, the more amenities, the more conveniences, the higher the price will be. If backroads land suits you, fine. Small parcels near towns may run $500 to $1,000 per acre. Waldo County in Maine is located on Penobscot Bay; total population is 27,000. As late as the 1960s you could buy abandoned properties for back taxes. Today is different. One farm, selling with 200-plus acres, six-room house, and barn for $6,000 back in 1960, changed hands twice. By 1971, just 50 acres without a house sold for what the entire property did ten years before.

Still, compared to land prices in southern New England, the foothills of the Appalachian Mountains in Virginia, or the Rocky Mountains, that price isn't out of line. As you look, don't be discouraged. Your search may require more effort than you anticipated, and the cost may be higher than you expected. Plot your course with a firm determination. There *is* a place for you. The secret is finding it and staking your claim *now*. Land prices are still climbing. Behind you is a surge of new pioneers, and they're just an anxious to make their move as you are.

One type of home that offers exceptional potential is the older "in-town" house. Many smaller villages have these larger homes, sold by widows and widowers who no longer need the room. With modifications, these can be made into two-season homes. You can enjoy the entire home three seasons. Come winter in northern areas, you simply retreat into a well-insulated wing and spend a cozy three to four months around wood-burning stoves. That may sound exaggerated, but many new pioneers have found that that system works. Granted, cramped quarters for several winter months is a bit much togetherness. However, look on the sunnier springtime side. You have a grand old house in which to enjoy life and operate your business ventures, providing you have checked the zoning rules before you buy. Some towns allow "professional" uses in residential areas. That usually means doctors, dentists, and lawyers, who can have offices. Your pottery, handicraft, mail order business, or similar nonretail business may be allowed.

Local zoning often prohibits retail sales, but allows you to make crafts or, teach classes, so long as you don't sell products. Older homes have the space for these activities and more.

You may prefer more land. Consider buying more than you need now. That land investment, as prices rise, can be money in the bank in years to come. Meanwhile, you can garden it, cut wood, or just enjoy the freedom of wide open spaces.

Land and homes are less expensive farther from the cities. That's a function of the "lack of city services," as the realtors express it. Actually, there are still bargains in the country and especially in smaller towns. Several reasons account for this. Farms have had to grow bigger to remain efficiently productive. Those smaller farms that couldn't provide a living for their inhabitants may have been incorporated into larger ones with some less-productive land left over. Often, farm families have moved to town, leaving their own older homes available for rent or purchase.

Millions of your fellow Americans have been programmed to expect and demand the ultimate in conveniences. Think how many of your friends and associates take for granted the latest kitchen appliances, zoned heating, easy access to shopping—total convenience available at a button's touch. That factor alone makes older homes with ample room for your crafts, hobby, and spacious, gracious living available for your purchase. Given the solid construction of many older homes, you can, if you are handy or willing to teach yourself the skills, rehabilitate older homes quite effectively.

One rule, passed along by many new pioneers, is to control your emotions as you shop for a home. Don't ever let that glimmer of appreciation, that sparkle in your eyes when you see a property that looks right for you, reveal itself to realtors. These professionals know how to capitalize on the slightest "oh" or "ah" to close a sale. Be calm, relaxed, nonchalant, and noncommittal.

Don't overdo the negatives, but do ask questions that reflect your concern that the home or property isn't what it should be. Perhaps a typical exchange would be helpful.

The realtor might say, "You can really make this home a showplace with a little work." Your reply might be, "But how do we know what we'll find when we replace these old walls? Maybe pipes about to burst! How old is the plumbing anyway? Is it copper or the old rusty iron pipes?"

The realtor might reply, "The owner had a new furnace and new plumbing put in just a few years ago." Find out when. Then ask whether, in this energy-short era, those old walls are insulated, and with what. It is your hard-earned money being spent, so get the facts you want. Don't look enthusiastic. Preserve your bargaining position.

Change subjects occasionally. Ask to see the fuel bills and the current price of fuel—gas, oil, or electric. Ask if any rate increases are pending. Look up at ceilings to see if new cosmetic painting jobs conceal problem leaks. Look out windows too. The neighbors may be nice, but a backyard auto repair shop can tell you zoning may be nonexistent. That may suit your purpose well if you wish to run a business from your new home, but you might get a junkyard next door next month.

Don't take the word of realtors that you certainly can have an office in the house or run a business in basement, garage, or barn. Ask to see the zoning regulations. Several new pioneers were astonished to learn that new ordinances forbade use of homes they had nearly bought for the purpose they had in mind, which realtors assured them they could do.

Many new pioneers found that a checklist, pulled together from the key points they listed mentally or on paper as they prepared to make their moves, was of great value. It enabled them to compare apples with apples and oranges with oranges as they discussed various areas and opportunities with their families. A written record also refreshed memories after hunting trips. It's difficult to remember which town had what facilities or which house was which after visiting several dozen areas and many homes in each.

Take along a camera, too, as you use your checklist to record key aspects of each town or home.

Your own personal checklist should reflect what it is you want in a home and in your new, independent career. You may wish to make a more refined list, adding weight in favor of certain attributes or assigning higher priority to particular values. How you make your checklist of desires is your personal option.

List all factors that you must know and would like to know. As time permits, fill in the answers, must-knows first. If you have children, a priority question will be the type and quality of school, the types of courses, the success of graduates in fulfilling their desires. Some school systems focus strongly on college-bound students; others have excellent strengths in vocational education. Find out which systems provide what you and your children want.

If you have especially gifted youngsters or, conversely, children with learning problems, ask whether their needs can be adequately satisfied. If you and your family enjoy sports, ask about school athletic programs and volunteer teams. Some areas emphasize athletics, while others are strong in Little League, hockey, or volunteer sports teams sponsored by local merchants. In a few places, backyard ball is sufficient. Sports-minded children may face desolate years if there are few outlets for what they've come to enjoy. Youngsters may be more set in their ways than you suspect, so be realistic. If you are a parent, consider all aspects of the proposed move from everyone's point of view.

Your sources of educational and athletic information are wide. Check with the school superintendent's office. Write to state departments of education—many reports are available. They provide details on costs of education, number of graduates, percentages going on to higher education. Review these reports with educators you and your youngsters respect.

When you visit an area, visit schools. Ask to talk with principals and teachers. Local papers carry stories about school board meetings; read them, and look through back issues. If a controversy is boiling, there may be a problem in that school system.

Write to state departments of commerce and industry. Write to chambers of commerce in areas you plan to explore as potential rerooting grounds. Collect literature, facts, and figures. Remember, of course, that tourist boards and chambers of commerces are not paid to downplay their areas, and maintain objectivity with regard to all promotional literature. From this, however, you can quite quickly tell about facilities, attractions, events that occur in areas. These can guide your search too.

Read the school and sports news with your youngsters. Look at the help-wanted ads, the business opportunity ads. Check the service clubs as well. Active service clubs usually indicate a spirit of community; people pulling together with pride in their hometown.

Read news about zoning, building, and environmental issues, and look for stories that mesh with your interest areas. Weekly newspapers have more in-depth comment by local correspondents. There may be craft and art exhibits that are of special interest, if that's your bag of tricks. You may find 4-H and farming news that tells you about the area's agricultural activities.

Remember, as you read the local papers, that many people sell their property or business directly without a broker. You can save real estate commissions when you buy direct, but be prepared to inspect things carefully yourself.

Do you have friends already living in an area you are considering for your new life? Have you or friends vacationed there? Ask around. You can pick up the most helpful tips from neighbors who have an aunt or cousin who lives and is employed in this area. Often these people lay the facts on the line. Their frankness may be surprising, and valuable.

When you arrive in an area, drive in it for about an hour without any preconceived ideas. Look at the land, the homes, the town, the schools. If you are a neatness nut or a colonial-heritage-inclined type, the look of the area will tell you whether people there seem to care about their property. Some areas that sound grand on paper may be in the second stages of decline. There may be bargains in property, but you may pay dearly if the town is suffering from what can best be termed rural decay.

Some new pioneers have moved their business ventures into areas that had a need for jobs. States may offer incentives to offset building costs, tax breaks, employee training grants. Look into these possibilities through state development boards, local chambers of commerce, and banks.

When you are in a town, visit several real estate agents. You may be leaving a town served by multiple listings, a cooperative system in which all brokers carry each other's property listings. Many smaller towns don't have this service. Brokers have exclusive listings. That means one may have just the place you want, but his competitor will never tell you about it if he himself doesn't have the listing or a split-commission arrangement. Many brokers, of course, have been in the area all their lives. Seek these out. Their knowledge of the territory is gained from growing up there; they know who owned what house or business and many other facts that you really need to know. Ask them about doctors and hospitals, taxes, and whatever else you think of. It's their job to sell you by providing what you need to know to make an honest evaluation of what they have to offer.

While in the town, visit the library and look up the history of the area. Talk to the librarian or the curator of the local historical society. These folks are often quite forthcoming and knowledgeable. They can provide answers to the same questions you asked of brokers and school administrators. From different answers to similar questions, you can make some sound judgments about the locality to determine whether it does meet your criteria.

Enjoy a few cups of coffee locally. Ask more questions. Be low-key but interested. If you have read up a bit on local news, you can open conversations of current interest. From that point, ask some of the questions on your list. Is there a bus that you could take to the airport or to a major city? Fine! Where could you get it? Where could you buy a new refrigerator? Where is the best place to shop for clothes? Who is a good dentist?

Ask about the best places to have lunch, dinner, early breakfast. Try some. Talk to the hostess, waiter, or waitress. Ask young people working after school how they like their school. Ask retirees what social activities there are. Be friendly, be yourself, be honestly curious and forthright. That's the best way to elicit genuine, to-the-point answers and information.

Once you travel beyond the city limits and leave suburban boundaries, you'll be surprised how friendly so-called natives are. They may spend an hour or so chatting happily with someone like you who is willing to listen. You can pick up news and gossip, facts and fancy. It's up to you, of course, to sort it out. But at this stage, you should be most intent on collecting as much information as you can about each potential rerooting ground.

Go to church too. Many churches have after-service fellowship coffee hours. Church members are often outgoing, eager to say hello and welcome new people to their town. The minister and his wife, the priest, the choir director, the deacon, or the head of the membership committee are key contacts. They are usually more than willing to answer questions and welcome you and your family to the town and their church.

Local pubs or bars are excellent places to meet the

natives. Bartenders and regular patrons can provide many details about an area that you can add to your notes. Remember, of course, that some people may be close-mouthed with strangers. When talking with them, a low profile, an honest, straightforward interest in their town can open avenues of answers to the things you want to know. There is a fine line between prying and a down-to-earth interest in the people and their area.

Example . . . One new pioneer was considering a rural Texas town. He and his wife sat alone at a local steak house, looking quite eastern in their attire and feeling they were out of place. An old rancher rose from his table and sauntered over to them.

"You're from back east!" he said with his easy drawl. They admitted to the fact. "Like steak?" the Texan asked. They admitted a fondness for good steak.

He invited them into the meat cooler, showed them some of his own beef from his feed lot, and recommended which cut they should try. Then the rancher returned to his table with his friends. The couple ate, enjoying the prime beef. When they asked for the check, the waiter said the rancher had already paid it.

"Just wanted to show you Texas hospitality," he grinned when they asked about his paying their bill. He invited them to sit down and introduced them around. They spent five hours getting acquainted with the people, learning about the area, and decided to stop their search right there. She now works in a clothing store in town owned by the rancher's cousin. He's a partner in a small but growing local investment business. Their income is lower, but their life-style is more gratifying than ever before.

Visit banks in your fact-finding forays around the countryside. Banks are always looking for new customers. Branches of larger banks may be staffed with transients, but local banks usually rely on long-established residents to build their local image. Ask about loans for business purposes, both long-range and short-term working capital if you plan to start a business or buy one locally. Shop for money as you would for a car or home. Rates vary. Establishing a line of credit is important for you as an unknown in a town. Make it clear, through your forthright inquiries, that you are for real, that you are down to earth and willing to explore the best ways to build your own venture in the area. You may be surprised at how readily a local banker may lay out facts and figures and provide just the answers and the help you need.

One new pioneer discovered that a bank held paper, the residual money due on a property loan that had to be foreclosed. The property was for sale to settle an estate. Asking price was actually below the appraised value, but to settle the estate immediately, a lower purchase price was agreeable. That saved six thousand dollars. With the banker's knowledge of the business and his willingness to help, the new pioneer owners were off and running well.

Another banker in a seacoast town held paper on a lobster boat. It was valued, with traps and hydraulic hauler, depth finder and radio gear, at $6,500. The owner had decided to forget about his boat and leave town. All the bank wanted was the $2,300 left on the note. A new pioneer now uses that thirty-six-foot lobster boat, with glassed-in sides he modified himself, as his art studio.

Before he made the move, he had worked fifty weeks each year as a commercial artist and took those precious two weeks vacation to sit on beaches painting watercolors. Today he paints for a living. His first painting hangs in the banker's office in gratitude for support when he first came to town.

Each scouting trip you make, make notes. As you look for homes or homesites, keep records. One family was perhaps more methodical than other new pioneers, but their experience can prove helpful.

Oscar Adolph made a scouting trip of three to four days every six to eight weeks. After each trip, he reviewed his impressions with his wife and children. Over dinner they discussed homes he had inspected, their location, and the towns in general. He answered questions about the schools, recreation facilities, shopping areas he saw. One of their priorities was four-season recreational opportunities. They all wanted water sports, fishing, hunting, swimming, boating. They also wanted to enjoy camping, hiking, mountain climbing, backpacking. They looked forward to winter sports as well as summer ones.

Since the younger sons didn't drive, they were interested in schools and friends within walking or biking distance from the home. In addition, they all agreed that rural isolation was low on their priorities list. They did want reasonable proximity to larger towns or cities for shopping, entertainment, occasional concert or theater trips. Two hours drive by car or bus was set as their outside limit. It was far enough away, they reasoned, to be out of suburban commuting areas. These criteria did eliminate some otherwise adequate locales.

On each of these trips, Adolph took one of the children along. After making such excursions over several months, he and his wife would fly or drive to an area to spend several days reviewing the best of what his scouting trips had left on their list. From Carolina's Blue Ridge Mountains to Florida's less-developed western coast, from the Shenandoah Valley to Lake Champlain in Vermont, they compared pros and cons of each area, each town, each home, and all the attributes of these with their priority lists.

Other new pioneers offer additional pointers from their own personal preferences. Intending to build a business from his hand-craft talents, a fifty-year-old former insurance executive haunted ship museums. His specialty-to-be was model ships. Museums and craft shows were focal points for him.

With children already grown, a smaller home was easier to find. He didn't need a large barn or studio since his work required little space. A double car garage suited perfectly. A used van proved efficient for picking up and returning ship models he restored and built.

Good land for growing crops was the key priority for another with pioneering spirit. He dug holes and probed soil to evaluate the depth of loam and topsoil. He tested soil samples for fertility. Level ground, easily turned and tilled, was important, as was ample water for growing crops. Zoning was a factor too, since many towns restrict construction of roadside stands and sales from homes. His search was further restricted by the cost of land, since he had a limited budget. Farm and forest zoning was one key. Inland old farms, away from tourist areas with their artificially inflated land values, was another factor. One of the most important elements in that family's decision was a comment they overheard in a supermarket.

They had asked why so many tourists were in the area at that time of year. "These aren't tourists," they were told. "These are leaf people." Leaf people, it turned out, were the difference between profit and loss to many of the local merchants. Tourists during summer pay the overhead and earn most merchants a small profit. Leaf people who come to see fall foliage add the extra profit for the year. That suited them perfectly. Fall is harvest season, the time when many leaf people would take home giant pumpkins, corn stalks; buy a not-quite-antique chair or old farm implements. Leaf people come back every year with friends.

Tourist areas may be a worthwhile choice for you. Each summer, tourists arrive in lake areas, along coastal towns and villages. They travel to the mountains and the desert. Most importantly, if you plan a business in a tourist town, these crowds of tourists bring their wallets and their purses. Even if you are intent on fleeing from crowds, don't drop tourist towns from your list of potential rerooting grounds. Tourists come and tourists go. They leave behind the cash that keeps you fed, housed, and clothed. They also leave you to enjoy the open space and your countryside in peace. For many parts of America, spring and fall are better seasons than summertime. You can have the best of both worlds . . . busy business for a shorter period and a time-off season to enjoy the new life that you sought.

Other areas have several tourist seasons. Skiing and winter sports have boomed across the country. Ski lodges depend, of course, on snowfall. Local businesses geared strictly to the weather feel the pinch when conditions in summer or winter aren't good. Several new pioneers studied weather statistics carefully over decades. They read old *Farmer's Almanacs* too. One decided that boat rentals coupled with motel rooms in summer and lodging, meals, cross-country ski rentals in winter would provide two-season income potential. It did. In the spring he paints, hikes, and prepares for summer tourists. Come fall, he hikes, hunts and prepares for winter ski season business.

Another couple split seasons and areas. Actually, he enjoys winter sports but her bones chill with the first frosts. They solved their dilemma with a split home and business plan.

In summer they operate a small marina, rent boats to vacationers, garden, and sell locally made handcrafts. Come late fall, they pack up their personal belongings and drive south. Their home is rented out completely furnished to schoolteachers and their families. As the sun warms his wife in Florida, he bartends part-time weekends and utilizes his mechanical skills in a lakeside marina in central Florida. They rent a house trailer there in a campground area. In the spring they head north again, leaving the campground owner to rent the trailer to others until they return next year.

As you plan your move, relax and think. The transition is easier than you imagine. Do take your time. Explore many areas and evaluate what they offer against what you really want to do and be. Many different areas probably offer opportunities to develop the life you desire. One couple ventured north on a trial basis, but bought open land in

South Carolina, which was their second choice area. North proved right, but looking down the road with energy in shorter supply, they're glad they own the southern land. In years ahead, they can easily transfer their mail order business to that warmer climate. All they need is a typewriter, a phone, a desk, and a packing room to continue business if the move south becomes a necessity.

Whatever phase you are in today, whether casually dreaming of the better life you deserve or actively plotting the final move of family and belongings, plan thoughtfully. Talk about your pending move with those you trust and love. Be logical, methodical, creative. Look far ahead as well as at the present and near future.

Then, when you see the light, when you feel that dawning realization that the time and you are in tune, pack up and make your move. There's no time like the present to begin your life as a new pioneer.

3/Get Ready, Get Set, and Go

The time has come, the decision is made, the scene is set. You've picked your place and are ready, willing, and able to go. Uprooting really can be quite easy, depending on how much you are still attached to your present life. Ah, there's the rub.

Moving isn't the pilgrimage of yesteryear. There are no Conestoga wagons to carry your belongings across desert and mountain pass, through wooded forest to your new frontier. More likely, you'll have thought ahead to a multipurpose van or other utilitarian vehicle. One of the distinguishing characteristics of new pioneers, it seems, is the preponderance of pickup trucks, vans, or similar vehicles among them. Many have shed their high-priced, high-powered cars for more realistically efficient vehicles. Some find that one multipurpose vehicle is sufficient until they get things going.

For some, unfortunately, uprooting time can be the most difficult phase of the transplanting process. You'll be leaving what you know, what you have become well accustomed to. Beyond that, you are moving in the direction of the unknown. Even if you have thought through every step, the pioneer trail can have its potholes and its perils.

You would be wise to accept old Murphy's law and make plans to surmount any and all obstacles that confront you. If something can go wrong, it will, the saying goes. One new pioneer typed that line and taped it to his dash, his kitchen sink, and his clipboard when he planned his move. Despite the fact that he had disliked the army and his years of military service, the long-forgotten training crept back into his consciousness.

As he put it bluntly, recalling attacks on well-fortified hills, "They told us in the army to always have a fall-back position. If we couldn't take the hill, fall back, regroup, and attack again. That old rule came back to serve me well."

Actually, as you begin the final move from a known to the unknown future life that lies ahead, some old rules should be kept in view. Except that all will not go as smoothly as you think. Think positively and lay plans to compensate for life's surprises.

One new pioneer's feet grew cold. He woke each morning in a sweat. What if the old house didn't sell right away? How could they carry two mortgages and for how long? Suppose the car suddenly needed major repairs; how would they get around in the new area? What if the products they made didn't appeal to enough people? Suppose, suppose, what if?

It's true you may face problems in your world ahead. Remember, you elected to make the move. Remember too the problems that you choose to leave behind. What you face, you can surmount. Problems are situations to be resolved. An older new pioneer had this thought, which he found helped him when things looked grim.

"If you can do something about a problem, do it and

don't worry. If you can't do anything, if it is out of your hands, don't worry, because there's nothing you can do. In general, 90 percent of the problems you may face fall into the prior category. Don't worry, dig in and resolve them."

One first step may seem obvious in your transition period, selling your present home. Think through that step cautiously. Perhaps a wiser move is to rent your old home with an option to buy. That provides steady monthly income for you and a chance to retreat if the pioneering world isn't what you thought it would be. Check with several realtors and have your home appraised. It may be worth more according to one realtor than another. Use three, add their quotes and divide by three to arrive at a realistic value. Always set a higher asking price, of course. You can always negotiate. In fact, 95 percent of home sales are negotiated, sometimes for what seems like endless weeks.

Begin searching through basement, attic, closets, garage. You'll find hundreds of things you really do not need. Moving goods costs money, so be hard nosed. Also, remember that your trash is someone else's treasure. If you have a large amount of furniture and odds and ends of fair value, consider an auction. Many auctioneers call themselves "colonel" and command a 10 to 20 percent commission of what they sell. But they usually command much better prices for the goods they auction off than you might ask at a community garage sale.

They'll estimate values and are much better at judging what items can really bring than you will be. Two neighbors, moving at the same time from one New Jersey community, took different routes in shedding excess worldly goods. Their experiences are worth noting.

One had an auction. The other organized a huge garage sale. Each watched the other's progress in ridding himself of old attic relics, basement junk, musty odds and ends that had collected dust for years. The wily auctioneer stirred the emotions of the crowd. He had advertised the sale widely, which attracted hundreds of eager bidders. On the appointed day, he whipped their eagerness into near frenzy.

Old rusty saws were auctioned at prices double the cost of new saws. Garage sale prices next door brought 50¢ to $1.50 each. Nicked bureaus and stained rugs brought lofty prices as the auctioneer extolled their values after refinishing. The scratched bureaus at the garage sale, brought $10 to $15 each, less than half the price the auctioneer attained.

You may not wish to hold an auction. Friends and neighbors may regard your selling your personal possessions as heartless. Perhaps an auction does hold potential embarrassment for some, but you may find it easier to overcome embarrassment when you bank the thousands of dollars an auction can bring.

These days, however, garage sales are the rage. Plan yours several weeks in advance. Advertise in local papers, listing the key items. Contact flea markets and antique dealers. They may spot special values. Many people come to garage sales in order to pay pennies for what they will resell in their stores or in their own monthly garage or lawn sales. One retired couple confided that they love to haunt flea markets and garage sales, barn sales, lawn sales, or anyplace household trash is offered. They've learned to spot the valuable items.

Each four to six weeks, whenever they have assembled sufficiently large piles of useless trash, they have another of their own periodic garage sales. Their rule of thumb, they explain, is to at least double, if not triple, the asking price. Their little backyard sales net them several hundred dollars every month. On occasion they also stumble on a rare find that brings a hefty sum. One desk without a leg, which they found later in an old barn and replaced, was rare indeed. An antique dealer, fortunately an honest one, did admit what it was really worth. That little lady's writing desk bought for $25 turned a tidy profit when sold at $1,150 through the antique dealer .

As you plan a garage sale, clean out every cranny in your home. It may seem strange, but the worst junk usually sells first and fastest. Old camp cots, torn and with broken legs, sold before one in perfect condition in one sale. Wire hoops used to support tomatoes brought $2 each.

Old jars, wood boxes, assorted nuts and bolts, nails and screws, a child's high chair, toys and games, old tools . . . all find ready buyers. Many new pioneers reported bonanzas from such sales. Cash ranged from just a few hundred dollars to several thousand in some cases.

Don't be too hasty. Some of those presently useless jars of nuts, nails, and bolts may be needed in your upcoming home-restoring work. In all likelihood, however, you can shed many items no longer needed and use the cash to pay part or all of the moving costs, with perhaps some left over.

Before you have your sale, if you prefer that over an auction, contact churches and other groups that have periodic rummage sales. They will send representatives. More important, make a deal with one of these groups to take all that is left over. They may buy it for one lump sum, or they may give you a written memo for the value of the things they take when your sale is over. You can write that charitable contribution off against your taxes. You also will be rid of all the trash that remains after the sale is done. That's a neat way to achieve your old home cleanup before you move.

Get bids from various movers. There are differences, especially if you plan to do much of the packing and moving of smaller items yourself. Investigate insurance for your move too. Most moving firms are covered, but a few extra dollars spent on insurance can cover unexpected damage that the fine print in a moving contract disallows.

Nearer moving time, your pioneering spirit rises. That's natural. Anticipation is usually greater than realization. Keep to a schedule. Cancel the appropriate utilities as necessary. Be certain you collect deposits you may have made but forgotten. See your postmaster. New rules allow forwarding of mail for just one year. A simple printed card will give your friends your new address. Bills somehow will find you even if you don't give companies your new location.

Pick up medical and dental records. Collect school records too, if you have youngsters. It is best to have as many of your personal vital records as you can in your own possession. Expect that medical files will be sent directly to your new doctor. As you finalize those last few weeks in the land you leave behind, it's up to you to pick up some of the pieces of your present life and cancel others. Utilities are notorious for continued billing unless you yourself have canceled such services.

Realtors, of course, can guide you in ways to cosmetically improve your house and clean up for the sale. Moving firms have excellent pamphlets that walk you step-by-step through a countdown of things to do before and up to moving day. Some real estate firms have branches nationwide or are associated with other independent agencies. They can help you scout areas in advance and provide well-documented data about localities and towns to which you plan to move.

If you must leave before your house is sold, curtains should be left on windows visible from the street, if possible. Timing devices to turn lights on and off are helpful too. The empty house will have a lived-in look, deterring would be burglars and vandals.

As the days dwindle down to a precious few before your move, don't bristle at assumed slights from people you believe are your friends. They have their problems as you have had your own. Don't crow about your good fortune. Those friends may stay. They may be as discontent with their lot in life as you were.

Your glowing predictions of your life to be, the great adventure and new freedom you pursue, are well and good for you. Others may wish to cut and run with you. There is no need to rub salt in the wounds of those who can't.

Another point from the pages of notebooks kept by several new pioneers is also worth considering. Predictions of glories in your new life may on occasion prove untrue. You may be the one who eats his words. A few who set out on their great adventure found the new frontier cold, harsh, and for them, uninhabitable. Dreams may fade and plans may crumble. It helps to have bridges you can recross if you must retreat to your former life. Not all have the stamina and staying power to remain among the new pioneers.

One man had seen his friends pull up their roots and opt for better lives. He too had become tired of his daily fare, commuting hours to the city and home at night. He began to hate his job. Petty annoyances grew into gigantic problems. Despite his expense account, his clubs, his new cars annually, he wanted out of that hassle-ridden routine. Unfortunately, he burned his bridges one by one, gleefully watching as they crumbled. He neatly cut all former ties, relishing every slash that severed him from those oppressive bonds.

Heading off to the golden glow of his new horizon, bridges to his former life still smoldering, he didn't fear the future. Unluckily, the economy of his chosen new career didn't fulfill his financial expectations. Sales did not materialize as he dreamed they would. In fact, disaster lurked behind each painful turn he made.

Back in the city, still licking a year's worth of wounds to both his ego and his bank account, he realized that many doors were shut. He himself had slammed them. Good jobs were filled. Interviews took time. For weeks he didn't realize that his bridge-burning joys had left a decidedly bad taste in the mouths of previous associates and customers. At last look, he was still on his feet, wavering but game to get back to some job that afforded steak and caviar again. In the process, he's eaten lots of crow. "It sticks in your throat and isn't very palatable," he readily admits.

As moving day dawns for you, grasp firmly all the loose ends that must be tied together. Before sunset you'll feel your spirits rise. Face forward as you seek tomorrow. Don't look back. Shed all regrets and leave them on your old home doorstep.

The open road lies before you. Move on. That new pioneer's life you wanted begins next dawn.

4/Settling In

The first dawn of a new pioneer's life may bring a storm. Rain or snow, sleet or hail, dazzling sun or foggy dew, nothing should daunt you on that most precious of all days. Look at the sky, the open fields, the woods. Look up and out and all around you at your new environment. This is the day that marks the turning point for all new pioneers. Absorb it, every minute that ticks past, every breath that you take, every bird that flies by and each breeze that rustles through your hair. This first day is the time to pause, to think, to meditate and contemplate and muse.

Play music if you like, or sit in solitude. There is much to do. It will be done. For today, let time wash over you. There are more important concerns this day; you and your future, the pattern you will set for years to come.

Among new pioneers, this first day retains its glow, its radiance, because it is the fulfillment of the promise they made to themselves.

"The first day we arrived, we found some old hay in the battered barn on our new property. Instead of unpacking immediately, we packed a picnic lunch. We spent that day sitting on the bales of hay, looking at the fields that stretched along the road toward town," Oscar Adolph recalls.

"It was a strange, almost exhilarating feeling. We saw birds and noticed cloud formations. We played a game with the youngsters, identifying clouds that looked like animals. I hadn't had time to play that game in years," he says. "Now, when a little problem pops up, we go back to the barn, sit on the bales of hay and think how to solve the problem. It sure beats the old office life."

Other new pioneers have picked their special spots. Most have a private place to which they can retreat and think, refresh their mind and spirit. That seems to be another aspect of life all share.

"My favorite spot is a bench I built near my animal pens," says Fred Pomeroy. "I've watched baby raccoons born, seen a mother bear raise a cub. I once spent an entire day watching turtles hatch and crawl out of their eggs. That may sound like little things to a lot of people. To me, it reveals the entire world as it continues despite itself. There, right in front of me, new life begins. Every time I sit and watch, I feel refreshed, clean and free again."

Lou Kashey also looks at nature regularly. He sees trees, boulders, views that give him pause. From his private observations, he envisions spaciousness as he designs another home.

"At last I have time to sit and think. Sure, there's work to do and if you want to eat, you have to work," he admits agreeably. "But it is important to look ahead, let your mind wander. Ideas can come at the most unusual time, but you must take the time to let your mind work as it will."

For Donna Sabaka, time to paint is her time to express herself. She now illustrates many books, inking in the tiny faces of animals peering from beneath a fallen log, or owls in a tree. Sometimes she sits for hours with her children, thumbing through nature magazines, talking with them and exploring the wonders of their young world. At times she takes her brushes and easel to a scenic local spot. There she captures on her canvas the old grist mill, fall foliage, reflections of a barn in its nearby pond. Those outings are her time to think and dream and put dreams on canvas in her calm new world.

"I hadn't fished in too many years," Phil Peters explains. "Now I walk down to the dock at our campground. Sometimes I get up before the sun or just as it sets. It doesn't really matter if the fish are biting. That's my time to think about the day before and the days to come. You don't need a bank account full of money to enjoy sunrise or sunset. Maybe I'll throw a pebble in the water and watch the ripples. My wife even found me asleep in my chair on the dock once and thought I looked the cutest then," he laughs. "She said I even had lost those worry lines in my forehead."

The first day of your new pioneering life can set the stage for those to come. Enjoy it.

Settling into a new routine, far away and foreign to the life you left behind, takes time. For some, establishing new roots, finding new friends, developing skills needed as a new pioneer may come easily. A few have found the process slow and somewhat difficult. Neighbors have seemed standoffish, more curious than friendly. That's natural. As you reroot in their neighborhood, those already living there may find your ways strange. They may need time to adjust to you and to what seems to them like strange habits you have brought along from your previous life.

Drinking coffee one morning in a local shop, a new pioneer began a daily round of visiting with natives. His idea was simple: He wanted to be accepted in his new life, make new friends, and blend into the slower-paced routine that he saw around him. As two natives prepared to leave, he heard their comments, perhaps said loudly enough for his ears.

"He seems nice enough, but it'll take some years to accept him 'round here," one offered.

"No, Charlie, you're wrong. Didn't you hear him say he's from New York? Probably take him more like forty years if ever before he gets accepted hereabouts. He's one of them city people."

Actually, the comments were a joke, he learned weeks later. But it did make him pause to take stock of his city ways. Those years of commuting, from suburban home to city job and back to country club on weekend, had marked him and bent his attitudes more than he realized. His citified sophistication set him apart. To blend in, he realized, he had to shuck off his "I know better" attitude. It may have earned him promotions in his corporate job, but when the septic system overflowed, he realized there were things he didn't know.

In many smaller towns there is a resistance to outsiders. Those whose taproots have been established for several generations may not take kindly to interlopers, intruders, or what some call newcomers. In some areas you may be a "newie." In other places, you're just from "away." It may seem awkward to you, being judged by your neighbors, but judging seems to be the prerogative of those who are native. Old eastern areas with heritages tracing back to the Pilgrim Fathers tend to be slower to accept new arrivals in their midst. Western states, filled as they are with newcomers, take the constant influx in their stride.

You may find that local residents view you with indifference, suspicion, even animosity. Buck up. Settling in, adjusting to them (and they to you) takes time. It helps to keep a low profile in the process.

Among new pioneers, women tend to have the hardest time adjusting unless they are involved directly in a new career. Children will meet friends in school and during after-school activities. Men among the new pioneers have greater access to people on the job and as part of routine activities around their new town. Women, if they retain a homemaker's role exclusively, may find the new life lonely.

"Talking to little people, your own children, as your only outlet for conversation all day gets to your nerves at times," one wife pointed out. "I had been accustomed to visiting with neighbors for coffee several times a week, playing bridge or just talking over our fence. When we left all those old friends behind, I hadn't expected building a complete new circle of friends would be so difficult. You don't just invite yourself into homes. It took months before I finally built a new group of friends."

Others, however, in fact most, found their transition more agreeable. One factor that helped all was their need for help.

"People in smaller towns have a long tradition of helping each other out," Fred Pomeroy notes. "When you're new and having trouble with your house or some problem you can't handle, it amazes me how quickly nearby neighbors will offer to pitch in to help you solve your problem. I mentioned a leak we couldn't find in the roof. Every storm the water didn't just trickle down the wall, it was a waterfall. I was crying about that problem at the local coffee counter one morning after spending three hours mopping up our living room," he recalls. "One plumber said he knew about that problem from a previous owner. He offered to call his friend who had worked with a carpenter some years back on renovation of our house. By afternoon both arrived, climbed into the attic with me and poked around until they found the spot where the water entered. One had some old caulking compound in his pickup. By later that afternoon they had helped me patch the roof. When I tried to pay them, they refused. 'Just being neighborly,' they replied and drove back to their homes."

Pomeroy's experience was echoed by many others. Natives may chuckle at your troubles, but they are quicker than you may expect to lend a hand when you are helpless. So, occasionally be helpless.

Another leaky roof—of an old house porch—gave Al Armstrong grief. With each snowstorm, water backed into the walls, soaking drapes and peeling new wallpaper off in sheets.

"I finally decided, after everything I tried failed, to swallow my pride and ask around. The neighbor across the road looked me straight in the eye. 'You got to shovel the first two feet of snow from the house wall off the roof.' he explained. I asked him why he didn't tell me that months before. 'Because you never asked me,' the native allowed."

Pomeroy decided to play dumb about other things, his septic tank included.

"I told my troubles to several people I met at the post office one morning. Clay ground won't take all that washing machine water, they told me. Every former owner had the same problem, but naturally the real estate people weren't anxious to pass that bit of misery along. I asked what they would do to solve the problem," Pomeroy recalls. " 'Call old man Ness,' they suggested. He, it seems, owned a gravel pit and specialized in adding laterals and building septic drainage fields. He solved the problem within a week."

If you're in a bind, ask for help. That simple point, obvious as it may seem, works wonders. Most new pioneers agree that asking for help was one of the secrets to their successful settling-in period.

It is basic human nature as well as a tradition in smaller towns to lend a helping hand to neighbors. It's also human nature to stand back and size up newcomers, to take their measure in good time. If a "newie" strikes a know-it-all approach, people just stand aside and wait till they climb down off their high horse, one local pointed out. God gave us our relatives, but we pick our friends, he added.

Almost every new pioneer in this transition period had anxieties or fears from time to time. Some worried whether they would be accepted, would find like-minded people whom they could enjoy as friends. Some, more outgoing and gregarious, made new friends immediately. For others, getting to meet new people and cultivating new friendships was a slower process. A few preferred to limit their circle of acquaintances, having made their move to escape the constant party rounds of their former life.

"Making new friends was a lot easier than we had expected," Bob Rouillard says. His wife agrees. "Our boys were active in sports. We went to games with them and met parents of their teammates and friends. I offered to coach or drive team members to practice sessions," he adds. "Their parents would stop to talk about a game and maybe stay to help me put up a few storm windows. We found we had a lot in common, beyond just the sports. We met other people who had left cities and suburban towns for reasons similar to our own. Today, we may have cookouts with a bunch of people. One may be a businessman, another a garbage collector, a truck driver, a local teacher. They're great people, down to earth, fun to be with. We've escaped that typical suburban social status snobbery. We can be ourselves as we always wanted to be, forget the pecking order of suburbia, and make friends with people who share our basic values."

Getting to meet people is actually much easier than you may expect. Even those who are naturally more private and less inclined to join clubs or group activities found smaller towns much more friendly and welcoming than they had anticipated. Benefiting from their collective experience, you may find it easier yourself to become acclimated to your new environment.

Church socials welcome new people willingly. You need not be especially religious, just friendly and relaxed. Local papers list bean suppers, pot luck dinners, bridge parties, and other mixers designed to bring people together. Many churches have public suppers regularly. Circulate. The food is tasty and often based on delicious prized recipes or just good meat-and-potato fare. Grange halls, scattered throughout America, VFW, Elks, and other groups also often have public suppers as fund raisers. These home-cooked meals are marvelous events at which to meet your neighbors, enjoy a laugh or two, blend into your new life surroundings.

Barbershop quartets and square-dancing clubs are just two of the typical events you can enjoy in many areas. Tickets usually are low priced. Cider, doughnuts, and old fashioned fun still exist at town political meetings. Take part, indulge your curiosity, attend activities you see posted on village bulletin boards or windows of local stores.

The couple doing do-so-do may be the local plumber and his wife, a farmer and his lady, or the people that run the antique attic down the street. They too, like you, respond to a friendly handshake, a warm smile, and kindly comments on the weather or the band.

There's a warmth that permeates small town and rural America. It never really left. Somehow, it seems, people crammed into cities and the frantic suburbs lose track of simpler things. As you step back in time, you'll find the people whose hometown you live in are more than willing to be friendly, helpful, and to share good times with you.

The Welcome Wagon and similar groups also extend a cheerful greeting to newcomers. Merchants, of course, find that a gift or discount at their store is one way to bring new customers through their doors. Go shopping, visit with the local merchants. Be a listener. You will find the change of pace refreshing and many people eager to spend time telling you about their area. The old cracker barrel may have disappeared long ago, but merchants still spin yarns and pass the time of day with any willing visitor to their stores.

"When you're new to a town, you don't know where to turn at times for service," Al Armstrong pointed out. "I spent every morning and some afternoons sipping coffee at various spots in town. Within a few weeks, I had begun to remember names and faces. I found that most of the people I met were as curious about me as I was about where to find a plumber, carpenter, dentist, electrician, and the dozen other specialists I knew that I would need, sooner or later.

"There they all were, sipping coffee with me. Judging from their conversations, I learned which plumber was most in demand, who charged the most, who was the most reliable. By seeing which carpenter hired or worked with which mason, you could size up the situation fairly well. Some were known for their patch and run work. Others were admired for their craftsmanship. Some had old-time pride in the work they did. Others readily admitted who was tops in his field. Getting to know these people over coffee, on a first-name basis, solved my problems. I knew who to call when pipes burst or the chimney began smoking badly."

All towns have their town halls where local business is conducted. But town committee men and women, selectmen and others in local government often compare notes and settle township business over coffee at their favorite luncheon spot. You can learn a lot about conditions at the grass roots while sitting at a coffee counter.

Lawyers rub shoulders with mechanics, bankers with fishermen, merchants with farmers. Try to rub shoulders with them yourself. In these energy-conscious days, some stores and eating spots are bringing back time-honored pot-bellied or wood-burning stoves. These once were focal points for impromptu town meetings. It seems they are indeed returning, a warming touch that can kindle new friendships for you in your new hometown.

One new pioneer recalls an amusing episode that occurred in his area. It wasn't so amusing for the person attempting to bring modern city ways to the town where he had bought the general store. For years, the central heating was an old wood stove. Counters were always cluttered, shelves were dusty. Customers charged what they bought and usually sat to jaw awhile with others.

The new store owner reorganized the counters, cleaned windows, removed the old stove and posted his cash and carry sign. He wasn't unfriendly, but to him business was to be business. Loitering didn't suit his turn of mind. He sent dunning letters to collect unpaid bills.

Within several months, customers drifted away. People paid their bills but began shopping elsewhere. Wives of older residents still chased their husbands out from underfoot, but they no longer had the old gathering spot where they could visit. That new storekeeper is back amid the bustle of a city now.

Residents recongregate around the reinstalled wood stove, and business for the newest owner is brisk again. He adopted a more relaxed attitude toward what he perceived was that town's mood. "You may be the owner, but you really must do business to a large degree in tune with the tempo of your town. If you become all business, your trade will drift away."

Service clubs are always looking for new members. Rotary, Lions, Kiwanis, and other civic-minded clubs offer a wide range of interesting and like-minded people. If you have been a member, reestablish your membership, attend weekly meetings, take part in their activities. You can become involved in raising money for a local ball park or cooking a chicken barbecue that will build a scoreboard for the high school field. Old-fashioned activities that you missed in the rush of commuting and city-oriented living are there in smaller towns. Pitch in. That town is your town now. What makes things really tick is the helping hands of volunteers, your friends to be and neighbors who take pride in each project they complete.

If you aren't sports minded, but have a talent that can add to the success of a youth organization, pitch in there too. Boy Scouts and Girl Scouts, 4-H and FFA, Junior Achievement and many other organizations are eager for additional leaders. The background you have can be of value to these groups. Just as important, you'll meet people more quickly and discover some who share your interests.

In smaller towns and rural areas there is strong respect

and high esteem for the worker and contributor. Undoubtedly, once you offer, you will be welcomed to serve on committees and to add your efforts to the benefit of whatever project is currently underway.

Some new pioneers expected that smaller towns would be devoid of so-called culture. They anticipated cultural shock as they uprooted their families from the "scintillating" life of suburbia. That just isn't so. Look around and listen. Community concerts, touring artists, traveling theatrical groups are on the road throughout America. The town hall or high school gym may not have the best acoustics, but the touring talent can be surprisingly appealing.

In Marlboro, Vermont, renowned artists from around the country and the world converge in summer to share experiences and their chamber music skills. The hills there resound with the sounds of music, in a more scenic setting than theaters of crowded cities provide. Residents of Biddeford, Maine, realized that the old opera house was still intact, acoustically sound, but standing vacant. An area-wide effort is restoring that old landmark. The Norman Luboff choir and other fine groups have been scheduled to perform there.

In Aspen, Colorado, Grants Pass, Oregon, Cedar Rapids, Iowa, there are as many cultural events and family fun activities per year as you will find in most cities. Theater groups need members, not just to perform but also to work behind the scenes, sell tickets, build scenery, help in many different ways. Volunteer, if you enjoy music or wish to audition for a part in one of these productions, or just get to meet new friends and share the pride of being part of that successful activity.

Portsmouth, New Hampshire, is not a small town or a city either. Yet there, in Prescott Park each summer, outdoor theater is offered free to thousands. Theater-By-The-Sea is funded by grants from the federal and state governments plus private contributions. Well-known actresses and actors perform side by side with local talent in a natural outdoor amphitheater for a thousand people every weekend. Families bring picnic suppers and folding chairs and share the entertaining fare all summer long. In winter, the theater offers shows in a renovated building among many that are being restored. Revitalization of smaller towns is being accomplished across the country.

In the old port area of Portland, Maine, what once were nearly derelict buildings have been renovated. New pioneers from many areas have set up shops, making and selling a wide diversity of arts and crafts. They've settled in, made new friends. They're working cooperatively to advertise the area, attract customers, and build their businesses as they live their new life-styles.

One new pioneer had fled a vandal- and burglary-ridden area. There he had kept doors locked, lights on at night and lived a fear-filled life. He was astounded when a neighbor arrived one morning with a backhoe on a tractor at his drive.

"Heard you had trouble with a water line," the neighbor offered. An hour later, trench dug, new pipe installed, he and the neighbor from two miles away were discussing frost lines, winter weather, and trout fishing, which they both realized they preferred over bass fishing. Several weeks later, he found four neatly cleaned trout on his back steps. He read the accompanying note to his wife. "Would have put them in your refrig, but you had your door locked," it said.

These days, he's fishing, snowshoeing, and wandering the countryside with his new-found friends. An avid gardener, he drops surplus corn, squash, and other produce on back steps. Invariably, he points out, he's invited in for coffee, pie, or whatever else is fitting for that time of day.

Another new pioneer was amazed by the attitude of teachers in the local schools. "Our children came home after the first week and seemed puzzled," he explained. "They said teachers stopped them in the hall and talked with them. Their teachers had invited them to join clubs, sports or other activities. Where we had come from, teachers were more interested in their union's campaign to raise salaries and reduce the hours they had to spend in extracurricular activities."

Settling in as a new pioneer can be exhilarating. You can step back in time to what were the good old days of people being human, neighbors being neighborly, friends helping each other enjoy the more pleasant life they wish to share.

The secrets of settling in your new life and finding the contentment you seek aren't all that secret. A willingness to contribute to your town's betterment, a friendly greeting, an ability to listen and tune in to the heartbeat of your community will make you welcome.

Be yourself as you want to be; relaxed, informal, accepting people for who and what they are. In many cases, you'll find that neighbors will be quick to knock on your back door. Some may drop in to visit with a pie or cake. Others may offer a jar of jam or a basket of their garden's produce. The old-time values are very much alive once you shed frantic city and suburban trappings.

Be a new pioneer in outlook, style, and spirit. From the first day that you arrive, let your instinct guide you. If you have the true new pioneer spirit, your roots will find fertile, welcome ground. The realization of your hopes, your expectations for a better life can be what you wish. The traditions of rural America are deeply rooted. They are there for you to find. Offer your friendship, your help, your willingness to share what you can with those around you. Those new pioneers who have successfully and contentedly rerooted have found peace in their new lives.

Some of their experiences may prove helpful to you in your rerooting plans and efforts. As new pioneers, they have willingly shared not just joys and successes, but also bumps, setbacks, sorrows. From reading about them, you can perhaps revise and rethink your plans. You may discover that new pioneering is not what you wish at all. More likely, their thoughts, desires, and accomplishments will be similar to the dreams you already have.

Having been a new pioneer, absorbing continually the stories of those who also have been and are, I welcome letters and visits from those yet to be. Together, looking at the future that we wish to build, we can create that better life we know must be.

5/Tales of the New Pioneers

By now, from what has been said about them, you no doubt realize that the new pioneers are a most engaging, special breed of people. They have often struggled to reach their decision to throw in the towel on old careers, even after pursuing them up many rungs of the ladder of success. During the months this book was being researched, many new pioneers spent literally days of their time providing background about themselves and their families. They reviewed and explored the reasons for their change in life-style so that you might learn from the steps they took in moving on in new directions that you may wish to follow.

From these individuals and their families, you will learn tips and guidelines to help you as you seek the new frontiers of life they have already sought and attained. Although many participated in providing points for this book and giving advice for specific chapters designed as guides to starting over, only a representative group appear in the chapters following.

You will find case histories of individuals and families in various stages of their new living styles. Some are well pleased and successfully rerooted; others are still in the transition stage. Some decided to embark on a new business venture at a pace and in a manner which they prefer, as contrasted to their previous jobs. Others are engaged in different livelihoods, ranging from mail order activities from their new homes to farming on a spot they carefully selected.

Their stories will no doubt afford guidelines for you to use as you plot your own course. A few, who prefer for personal reasons not to embarrass previous employers or old friends they left behind, asked to have their names changed, which has been done. Their stories, like all the others, are true representations of their feelings, changes, lives, and goals.

In the months that I spent preparing this book, it all became increasingly obvious to me that most new pioneers shared a similar philosophy. For the most part, they believed that there had to be a better way for them to live their lives. And they believed in taking the responsibility for making their lives work in the ways they had decided upon. So, in the tales of the fifteen new pioneers and their families whom you are about to meet for the first time, it's just possible you'll recognize yourself. All of us at one time or another have longed for a change in our lives. Perhaps the sagas of these bold spirits will inspire you to translate that longing into action—and to further expand the ever-growing chain of Americans who are starting over.

6/Larry Benton—
From Audiovisual Specialist to Organic Farmer

In the world of big corporations, executives have many ways to guide and increase the progress of their subordinates. Through company management seminars, aided by advice from outside business consultants, and in courses taken at leading universities, junior executives are trained in efficient, effective, productive management techniques. A sure way to ensure upward corporate mobility is to be the bearer of a Masters of Business Administration degree. With it, you usually can launch your career at a fairly high level in a company rather than waste time in junior management trainee programs.

Companies have learned how to spot the potentially bright lights who eventually can assume top leadership positions. They have devised an array of screening tests, questionnaires, and personal interview techniques that reveal who has the talent for future corporate management. In many cases, these tests do indeed separate wheat from chaff, managerially speaking.

Larry had his MBA from a highly respected university. His undergraduate days were memorable: Phi Beta Kappa, Magna Cum Laude, member of student council, letters in two sports. He was a fraternity man, and according to the evaluations of his professors, was a comer in the world of business.

Letters of recommendation opened doors for interviews at several of *Fortune*'s 500. He had his pick of offers, a clear shot at top spots.

Within five years, his communications specialty had proved its worth. From sales conventions to board meetings, from management training seminars he organized and supervised to stockholder meetings, Larry Benton communicated well. His multimedia, audiovisual presentations illuminated his company's strongest points. They created the necessary awareness and appropriate reaction from the audience.

He was effective verbally and visually. His slide presentations, product movies, convention booths, even point-of-purchase packaging displays won him compliments and awards. He moderated meetings with product managers and advertising agencies to help plan marketing strategy and ad campaigns.

Larry was a natural team player. His test scores revealed that aptitude, and his superiors' reviews for promotion directly resulted from his understanding of the people-persuasion methods needed for upward movement through the ranks of management.

"I could focus on key product points, put them in the spotlight, get customers to blink their eyes more frequently when they saw our products in the stores so they would buy ours over the competition's," he recalls. Color, design, a clever combination of posters, cartons, and self-service displays were other strengths that earned him recognition.

"Salesmen need motivation, incentives, a good goosing to keep them selling all the time the way they should to meet their quotas," he points out.

"Some people are motivated by money, which can be bonuses, commissions, or promotions to a higher salary. Others are looking for their own district, region, or area to climb into sales management jobs," Benton explains.

"But others, they need more subtle motivation. Incentives from a chance to win a vacation trip or a fur coat for their wife or girl friend in a sales contest, to membership in a country club for the two best salesmen of the year. There are hundreds of ways to motivate people. My job was to get the message through loud and clear to the sales force and right through to their bedrooms too. We had campaigns aimed directly at the wives, or husbands, if the wife was on our sales staff. The theory is quite simple . . . get the one at home to put pressure on the spouse to keep him selling."

Also under Benton's jurisdiction in the communications campaigns were internal communications. He could aim a letter through the front door of a salesman's home that had most wives eager to see their husbands back in the field early Monday morning to reach the goals the company expected. Benton persuaded and cajoled and motivated well.

Conventions, meetings, and meetings to plan future meetings are also part of the business world. Some salesmen have resistance to conventions that require weekends away from home; wives especially may resent them. Women can be peculiar that way.

Benton offered family trips, based on an airline's successful "take-me-along" campaign. Wives were wined and dined and made to feel part of the company family. After all, a contented salesman with a happy spouse could function more effectively with no family problems on his mind.

Show and tell and sell, whether products or company philosophy, was Benton's forte. His wife hardly ever balked when he caught the Sunday plane to one more convention where his audiovisual skills required him. If he played the expense game well, he could add another $2,000 annually to his substantial salary.

"I missed some weddings of friends, a funeral or two which I didn't really want to attend anyway, and lots of dull school plays and PTA get-togethers," Benton recalls. For him, corporate life was up, up and away.

He taught courses too, for younger members on the company's teams. He showed them, for example, how to arrange displays in retail stores, how to charm store managers to gain more prominent positions for their firm's products.

"We hammered at the same point in different ways. Get our goods at eye level where the customer could spot them easily. They should be able to pick our products off the shelf without stretching up or stooping down to reach them.

"I really enjoyed the job and didn't have any thoughts of leaving," he explains. "A few things bugged me, like questions the salesmen asked about the sugar content of some products and the rise in tooth decay, or the perennial one about junk foods that had no real nutritional value. We had the answers. More cities were fluoridating water to stop tooth decay. Dentists had to live too! And," he chuckles, "the sweeter the food, the sweeter the profits. That always got a laugh."

Other companies among the competitors also had their impact in the marketplace. Their food products were quite similar, actually. Benton didn't eat them. He didn't buy or eat his firm's products either.

"But what finally really began to bug me was my kids," he remembers. "They watched the TV and went shopping with my wife. They were always getting her to buy some product that had no great food value. It just was packaged right. Or the display got to them. Some even tasted good, I guess, because the kids kept putting it in the cart every time they were in the supermarket.

"My wife began nagging the kids to eat what she had

cooked because it was good for them. I heard that a thousand times. We threw more good food away, expensive stuff, because the kids ate all the other stuff, a lot of it. My wife was reading books on child persuasion, trying to find ways to convince them that they should eat a balanced meal, natural foods, things that were good for you. The kids always had an answer . . . if my wife tried to explain that the sweet stuff wasn't really good for them, they had the perfect answer . . . in a question. They asked 'Why does Daddy sell it?' "

Benton had heard the same arguments at breakfast and dinner month after month. His son learned from his daughter, who had learned from her older brother.

Three years ago, Benton and his family spent a week's vacation at a farm in New Hampshire. It was a chance to show the children where milk, eggs, bacon, wool, and lots of other things originated. His children were fascinated. Milk came from a cow, not the plastic bottle. Eggs materialized in a nest, not in cartons at the supermarket. Vegetables grew in the ground, not in plastic bags.

"It was like a revelation," he says. "They actually ate the food, even asked for seconds. That started me thinking, I guess," Benton admits. He and his wife, with their children, helped with farm chores. That was part of the fun at the farm. They milked a cow, fed the chickens, picked berries, rode the hay wagon. They ate, hungrier than usual after a day in the fields and gardens.

"When the kids were in bed," he explains, "my wife and I talked with the farm owners. They had been living in suburbia in New Jersey when he worked at an ad agency in New York. He had pulled the plug and become a farmer. We compared notes. In a way, I was in the same game. We were about the same age. We had interests in common, but he was in the country. His kids loved it, and I was in the city trying to get my kids to stop eating the things I was promoting.

"The kids didn't want to leave the farm. Actually, I

didn't either, but we had to get back for school opening and I had more conventions to attend."

All that year, Benton and his wife read up on gardening. They reasoned that if their children enjoyed growing vegetables and eating them, they should have a garden themselves at home. They read about organic gardening, subscribed to an organic gardening magazine, visited the famous organic farm in Emmaus, Pennsylvania. Twenty books later, the idea of buying a farm and going organic was entrenched in their minds.

Today, after several years farming their own land, Benton and his family seem to be thriving.

"One day at a convention, I realized that I didn't really believe in what I was doing. The kids did, they ate the stuff. My wife and I sat down to do the taxes one night. We paid them to the federal government, the state, the city. We paid income and property taxes. We paid taxes on clothing, on food in restaurants. We paid taxes on the car, the refrigerator, the TV. When I added it all up we were paying thousands and thousands of dollars in taxes."

Taxes on their forty-six-acre farm are one quarter of what they had been paying for two acres in suburbia. New Hampshire is a notable exception among the fifty states. It has virtually no taxes. They are paying property taxes, of course, but few others. If you drink, smoke, or gamble, you pay the freight. New Hampshire has its lottery, dog races, state liquor stores. Much of the state's revenues come from what has been called "taxes on sin."

Organic gardening, and farming too, have become popular in recent years. Benton reasoned that since there was a market for organically grown foods, he could tap his talents for promotion and salesmanship to build a market for what the family grew.

The year they invested most of their savings and the income from sale of their home into the farm, Benton and his wife applied their energies to restoring the deteriorating house and building their roadside market.

"We visited a lot of organic gardeners and roadside markets," Benton explains. "Many were sloppy. From my background, I knew what was wrong. The objective of any display should be to reinforce the most favorable sales features of your product. Good health, nutrition, naturalness were the key factors in organic produce. Sloppy displays were bad. Eye appeal is so deeply engrained in the public's mind that we couldn't ignore that fact, even if the apples we grew had some bruises."

The Bentons selected a natural look as the style for their stand. They scoured the countryside for old baskets, tubs, containers. Flea markets, garage and barn sales, antique shops were the best sources. They collected old containers used for picking apples and fruit, wood containers formerly used to ship produce.

As they drove backroads, they spotted barns about to collapse. They marked these locations on their map. Several months later, they had contacted owners, bought the old structures for next to nothing, dismantled them, and saved the best wood. Useless boards were saved for stoking their kitchen stove.

Old barn sidings salvaged from the dismantled barns were scrubbed and left to dry naturally. This wood was used for their stand and its shelves, plus more containers for produce. The baskets, boxes, jugs and containers added to the naturally organic look they wanted to achieve. Signs were hand lettered carefully, with old-time lettering that had a feeling of nostalgia.

Beams from old barns and extra boards weren't wasted. The Bentons paneled their family room with natural barn boards. Hand-hewn beams now decorate their kitchen and hall and serve as mantels for their fireplaces. Their public rooms, where visitors share a cup of coffee, enjoy a home-cooked, organically grown meal, and buy their goods, have a feeling of rustic America.

They grow much of their own food as well as what they sell. And sales have been climbing rapidly since the first year they set up their roadside market. Within that first year, the Bentons began contracting with other organic gardeners who had greener thumbs than they did. That produce also moves quickly and profitably across their roadside counters.

"Many people can grow things better than we can," Benton admits. "But I know how to present the produce and make it really move."

There's a bit of showmanship in what they do. Their signs convey the feeling of naturalness. Produce is clean; displays are neat. They have books about organic gardening for sale and little mottos on the walls. One reads, "You Are What You Eat, Naturally." Another says, "Our Produce Is Naturally Tastier."

In Maine a long-established barrel and tub manufacturing firm is experiencing a revival. Benton bought a load. Customers remarked so often that they wanted to buy Benton's vegetable display containers that he began buying and selling the barrels and tubs. That added a new income source.

"Display had been one of my strongest assets," he smiles. "I knew where to shop for the most modern, easy-to-ship, best-lit displays for conventions. Here I am now specializing in the oldest displays I can find."

Larry Benton is also in the lumber business. He dismantles barns in his off season, late fall and winter. If you travel in New England, you may someday see his beat-up old farm truck lurching down a country lane, loaded with what looks to be piles of ancient lumber. It is another golden source of income to the ex-audiovisual expert.

The only acquaintance the Bentons had with antiques was a few elderly bureaus and some chairs handed down from grandparents when they first married. Today they have their favorite old furniture that they will not sell. They also shop in their off-season travels for antiques. Two rules apply in their fall and winter searches.

First, the Bentons look for furniture that is similar to that for which they receive the most compliments.

They have a book in which they write down comments from summer visitors. They keep count of which type of furniture is most wanted. That's rule number one: Buy only the pieces that can be resold fast, avoid the others. Rule number two says, Don't get too attached to the sales merchandise.

The Bentons also deal in old containers and parts of their constantly changing produce displays. They sometimes buy a load of old apple crates for 50¢ each and truck them home. Customers cart them away at $2 to $3 each, depending on condition. The older ones bring more money.

Barn boards, weathered by years of wind and hail, snow, sleet and summer sun are stacked neatly near his barn. Buckets of nails retrieved from the boards are for sale, some modernly round, many antique square-cut ones.

"Old barn boards are big business," Larry Benton says with a nod toward his piles of planks. "People go nuts about them. They see our family room and buy a load to panel their own den or family room. They buy the beams to make their ceilings look old fashioned. They even make furniture with them."

Benton sells the salvaged barn boards to selected contractors in the cities too. He gets top dollar. It may cost him from $100 to $400 to buy an old barn before it falls down. He figures dismantling it may take a week. Cost of the boards that aren't too far gone averages 10¢ to 20¢ per foot. He sells them for $2 per foot and more for those with all the patina of age and naturally weathered nostalgia worn into them.

Firewood is selling well too. As more homeowners convert old fireplaces for use of wood-burning stoves, well-seasoned hardwood is in demand. Benton fills that need too.

Seasoned wood at his stand sells for $55 per cord. Smaller bundles, tightly tied with stout hay bailing cord, sell for $5 each. Delivery costs more, he reports. A truckload delivered to customers on the fringes of Boston brings

$100. Those trips don't really pay off, but the Bentons like to enjoy a play or concert now and again. Boston isn't that far away.

On occasion, former associates swing down his lane, a country blacktop road that has sufficient summer traffic to keep his market busy. Some still ask his advice about displays and audiovisual presentations. He obliges gracefully. It's good for business.

The barn boards, containers, boxes, baskets, and other items are for sale. Displays designed by Benton exist today in department stores, garden centers, and elsewhere in and on the fringes of large cities. He remembers well the huge budgets that he spent for point-of-purchase displays. As a supplier now, as well as a part-time designer when asked to be, he counts another source of income for materials, plus extra dollars earned working with local carpenters to build displays that he ships away.

Even the Benton children are active in the family business. They cut and split firewood. They harvest crops and set up displays at their roadside stand. They make up signs and paint them.

In suburbia, one pet was all the Bentons had, a black Labrador. They had it spayed to avoid problems from neighborhood wanderers. Today they raise black Labs for fun and profit. A good litter brings in $1,000 or more, depending on the number of pups whelped.

Several sheep keep the lawn cut neatly. They make a tasty meal, from lamb chops to Irish stew. Their offspring mow the lawn next year. Pigs are essential on an organic farm. Surplus crops, overripe vegetables, unsold produce keep the hogs well fed. An old goat that their daughter obtained in a trade with a neighbor pulls an old wooden wagon around a field along the road. That spectacle stops traffic on weekends. Gail gets 25¢ per ride in the wagon. While the visiting youngsters enjoy their rides, their parents shop for vegetables and fruit.

Looking back toward Boston, Larry Benton believes he

and his family laugh a lot more than they did. They joke together about the mistakes they made the first few years of their new life. They laugh while putting up their jams and jellies, many from the wild berries that grow randomly alongside their barn. They get nearly hysterical remembering how they felt when they examined potato vines and their children couldn't find any potatoes until they realized that the spuds grew underground.

"We stepped back in time," Benton believes. "It was good timing. We stepped back just when the public was becoming more aware of their past and heritage. The good old days are being thought of fondly. Nostalgia was marketable. My background helped me channel the ideas and talents I had in a new direction, to sell what we grew or picked or cut or whatever.

"In many ways, we've been lucky. The time was right, the mood of the country, the consumers were on our side. Maybe we couldn't have done it another time. Maybe what we did wouldn't work for another family," Larry states.

"It took a lot of pitching in together, something we never really had time to do before. It brought us together more. And," he adds, looking at one of his daughter's mottos on the walls, "it's all natural for us today."

7/Eva Horton—
From Housewife to Wood Stove Importer

Her youth in war-torn Norway during the Nazi occupation was spent around a wood stove, stoking the fire, gathering wood, or just keeping warm in the frigid winters. She had, in those days, no time for thoughts about the future or for any dreams of becoming a successful businesswoman. Survival was the topic in those days, and how to drive the Nazis back into the sea. In her family's home, when she was seven to twelve years old, they had several efficient wood- and coal-burning stoves. During wartime, fuel was scarce. These stoves that warmed her well made a lasting impression.

During the years spent in America, raising a family, working constantly to help her husband get his degree and pursue his career in oceanography, Eva still had little time to think about or plan a business career for herself. There were gardens to tend, food to cook, children to raise, a husband to help in his efforts to establish his career.

Winters can be severe in New England, where the Hortons lived. Snow piles deep and winds howl, building drifts that can keep you housebound for week after icy week.

During her early years of marriage, Eva worked at various jobs to help provide income for the growing family. She was a liberated woman long before the term became fashionable, if working hard means being liberated.

"I've vacuumed at least 642 miles of carpet, served more than 20,000 meals to the family, baked my own bread, made my own wine, grown our own vegetables, caught our own seafood, and I was the best customer the Salvation Army Store had," she recalls.

"When you figure 365 days multiplied by three meals a day, multiplied by the number of years, you can add it all up to a lot of cooking, washing, and cleaning up," Eva points out.

Keeping a house, feeding a family, growing food, and doing all the usual housewifely chores kept her occupied for many years. She also did a lot of thinking.

"I nursed the babies, and during those hours I thought about many things."

In the family home she also raised golden retrievers. Their early years of marriage were busy ones. In their two-bedroom house with three children and about eleven dogs, give or take those she sold, Eva supplemented the heat with wood in a Heatolator fireplace.

Eventually the family bought a farm retreat in Andover, Maine. There, too, she cooked, cleaned, heated with wood, and thought a lot.

"Fireplaces are inefficient," she points out. "They can throw out what seems like a lot of heat, but actually they can only give you about 10 percent of the heat that is in the wood. The rest goes up the chimney as heat and smoke . . . that just is not efficient."

In 1972, Eva Horton had been through some chilling times. Winter in the north woods can be a cold experience in many ways. Remembering her youth in Norway and the warm glow of the wood-burning stoves, she wrote to her family there. In due course they sent her a Jøtul wood-burning stove, a #602, she recalls. It was cast-iron, air-tight and burned wood more slowly than conventional stoves. That meant less time to gather and cut wood. Because the stove was efficient, with baffle systems inside to burn not just wood alone, but also the volatile gases that normally escape up a chimney in the burning process, it gave off more heat.

Friends and neighbors came to visit. They marveled at the heat the little stove could radiate into the room. Eva enjoyed entertaining, even on a limited budget. She had been a gymnast years before and a teacher of track, physical education, and dancing when the family lived in Rhode Island. That background, and a love of life, friends, and people in general kept her smiling when times were tough.

"As friends saw the stove and compared it to the minimal heat they obtained from their open fireplaces or Franklin-type wood stoves, they too wanted a more efficient stove for their homes. Wood-burning stoves are no big deal in Europe," Eva remembers.

"Wood stoves are a way of life there, where most homes had no central heating when I grew up. Wood and coal were the commonly used fuels. Families heated their cottages and even large homes with wood." Despite the fact that Americans have been accustomed to oil, gas, and electricity as easy, convenient heating, Eva thought there might be a good response to sales of wood-burning stoves. Many of her friends and her husband's friends seemed interested in them.

In 1972 she sent away for another stove, then another for friends who wanted to buy them for supplemental heat in their homes. As more people saw the stoves and were warmed by them, their appeal grew naturally.

"That was about the time when many people were concerned with the environment. There was a feeling that a return to self-reliance was overdue," Eva recalls. "*The Whole Earth Catalog* seemed to have wide appeal to people of all types. And," she adds, "people were becoming aware of the energy crisis and the increasing cost of fuel to heat their homes."

She watched the enthusiasm of people for her stove and calculated that there might really be a strong sales potential for this type of stove in the United States. After all, such stoves were an accepted fact of life in the Scandinavian countries and in much of Europe. Although they didn't look like the typical American pot-bellied stove, the Franklin or old-fashioned cast-iron kitchen range of rural areas and bygone days, they had many more advantages, she reasoned.

She wrote to her father in Norway who knew the people involved with one of the world's best wood-burning stoves, Jøtul Stoves, and thought even harder about the potential. Yes, the company was interested in selling stoves. She spent long hours estimating how many she might sell and how that might help the family income. At that time she had no real figures on which to base her sales estimates. Even if she had been trained in business, there was no real way to predict the future sales of what some people thought was a funny-looking little wood stove.

"They're cute," a friend had said, "but are they really any good?" Eva knew they were.

During her youth and the years of her marriage she had learned to improvise. She was a self-starter, she had realized. When the family lived in North Carolina she had initiated an area-wide recreation program. With a mere $1,500 budget she started twenty-seven different activities to serve many hundreds of youngsters in that area. She also recruited forty volunteers for the program.

As the letters flew from Maine to Norway and back in 1972, Eva felt her entrepreneurial tendencies rising. Other people had begun businesses, why couldn't she, she asked herself. She had proved effective at organizing people.

Some friends urged caution. After all, they pointed out, she had no business training, no experience. Starting a business of your own with little capital, no experience, no background with which to convince bankers when you needed to borrow money—all this was against her. She was, after all, one person pointed out, just a housewife.

That comment and others like it may have been the trigger that propelled Eva Horton into the business world. One thing was certain. She had done many things, held jobs of all descriptions, part-time. For many she had had no background, but she had done them well. She had a good mind, determination, a profound belief in her abilities, and perhaps the most important ingredient necessary for success in business: desire. As friends had said about her, "Eva doesn't know the word can't. When she takes aim at something, she goes after that goal with all her energies." Eva focused on stoves and a career. She focused well.

Her ship came in, in 1973. Actually, it was typical of Eva Horton that a Norwegian ship brought her first delivery of Jøtul stoves. The shipment included models #4 and #118, which she had thought would be the best to sell for their appearance and heating ability.

"I felt jubilant," she recalls. Jubilation with Eva Horton was like jubilation in few other people. Although she hadn't yet opened a store or even had a place of business that could display the stoves, her enthusiasm was contagious. She called every newspaper she could find.

"My stoves have arrived," she told startled editors. "Don't you want to get pictures of them?" Some did, some didn't.

Normally business firms hire advertising agencies and public relations experts to tell their product story to the press and to prospective buyers. Eva didn't worry that she had no professional talent to do this product introduction campaign. She kept calling editors to extol the virtues of her stoves.

Editors, being susceptible to good news stories and invitations to press parties, began responding to her invitations. She put on her best, authentic Norwegian national costume. Thus in keeping with the tradition of Norway, her background, and the stoves as well, Eva made a charming hostess.

"I threw a party and invited everyone I could find that might be interested in my stoves," she relates. "They might be reporters or editors or just people who would buy a stove. I needed exposure." She was determined to be noticed.

At that point in time, several factors focused public attention in her direction. The old, run-down waterfront area of Portland's harbor was in the process of having its face lifted. New shops were being opened featuring arts and crafts. Buildings were being renovated and trees replanted. Many people had foreseen that old areas could be revitalized in their towns and cities. Portland was ready, willing, and able to revitalize its Old Port area. The old look, nostalgia, a feeling for the past, all were coming together to set the right mood for her business venture.

The other fortuitous factor that buoyed her spirits was the arrival of America's energy crisis. Prophets of doom had predicted an oil shortage for several years. Americans, as they often do, shrugged off the thought of such a problem. Their homes were warm, their food plentiful, gas for cars cheap. Good times would certainly continue rolling on.

A meeting of Arab oil-producing nations changed that rosy picture. Few saw the writing on the wall. Few listened to the reasons for the coming crisis. Fewer still were prepared for it when it came, and scarcely anyone believed it was real or would last for any time at all.

Eva's calculations, that wood stoves would be a coming trend, were soon to be proved correct. How correct was something even she in her wildest hopes or most ambitious projections could not foresee.

Her first display for the attractive little wood stoves was in a leather craft shop along a street in the area being rebuilt as the Port Exchange, the "Salt of the Earth" store.

Eva herself drove the battered family stationwagon to the pier. She sweet-talked workers there into helping her load the stoves into the wagon, then drove three blocks from the pier to the store.

There, the stoves competed for attention with handcrafted wall hangings and leather goods on display. People bought them.

A few sales don't make a business, she realized. But she talked with customers, discovered what they wanted, followed up to learn more about their reactions. Her enthusiasm was continually contagious. More customers came to buy.

"When I threw a party at the Sheraton Hotel," remembers Eva, "even the governor came, because he was having a meeting at the same hotel. But he stopped in and that made my day and the party too."

With her boundless energy, convinced her ship had indeed come in at last, Eva went shopping. She still had no recognized business experience or management background, but her intuition told her that the future would glow brightly for her.

"I had been a housewife, as people reminded me," Eva recalls. "And I had shopped carefully for everything I bought, from food to clothes. I bought clothes at the Salvation Army Store, turned them inside out and made them into new clothes. One thing I knew how to do was shop."

Eva applied the same principles when she went shopping for a banker, an accountant, a shipping agent, a customs broker. She can be brutally blunt or disarmingly charming. She asked them what they could and would do for her.

"Banks are money stores. You should shop around for the best buy on money when you want to borrow it," she believes.

"There's competition among banks to attract customers. There is competition among shipping agents, accountants, and all types of businesses."

Eva shopped around to get the most for her money.

The long years of frugality, the experience managing tight family budgets as a "mere housewife" had given her a business experience that isn't taught in college or business management courses. She understood the bottom line better than many with Masters of Business Administration degrees. Eva had always known how to use a sharp pencil when she went shopping.

She could find bankers who were willing to guide her, give her sound advice, arrange loans on a mutually agreeable basis. She interviewed them and others who could provide the services she needed to develop her import business.

Some may have been astonished that a "mere housewife" would ask such pointed questions, could grasp ideas and accept suggestions so quickly and put them to immediate use. If they were astounded, they came to be fully aware that Eva Horton was far more than a housewife. Her ingenuity and enterprising talent were in full bloom. Today she is harvesting the fruitful rewards of her efforts.

When the next shipment arrived, she called not just newspapers, but radio and TV stations too. Some came. Her stoves were seen by potential customers in TV-land. More prospectives buyers read about them in their newspapers. Other media picked up the excitement and the story. Free publicity was paying off.

Some customers wanted to be retail dealers. Eva had already thought through that stage of her planned business expansion months before. She had looked far ahead and taken the most direct approach. She had the audacity to ask the Jøtul Stove Company to give her distributorship for the entire United States. They responded to half her request; the half of the United States east of the Mississippi River was her domain.

Her first year in business began with two stoves. The next shipment of 250 was sold out. And she could have sold them many times over. She realized her potential was a hot one. That first year, she sold 5,000 stoves. She answered letters, wrote orders, supervised shipments, appointed dealers while scrubbing pots and cooking meals. The future, she saw, was glowing even more brightly.

Today, Eva Horton is president of Kristia Associates, the company she started around her own wood stoves in the chill of winter. She imports full shiploads of stoves, from small one-room heaters to those that can warm an entire house. She organized her own advertising agency to serve her company and other clients too. She is diversifying into related products and writing books as well.

During 1976 she traveled through Norway, other Scandinavian countries, and England. Her goal was to learn more about wood heating and examine other products that she might add to her line through her expanding dealer network. By this time, several hundred dealers were selling her Jøtul stoves. Her initial sales had multiplied. The manufacturer had appointed her the exclusive distributor for their stoves throughout the entire United States. Sales were hot and getting hotter.

After interviewing hundreds of people in her European travels, she spent time on the rooftops of homes across Europe too. Eva was determined to learn the business of wood stoves, not just inside the home, but all the way up the chimney as well.

"In Europe, chimney sweeps are a part of daily life. They make their daily rounds across rooftops to clean chimneys. When you use wood stoves constantly, chimneys need cleaning," she points out. "There were few people in the chimney-sweep business in this country. It seemed logical, with all the stoves we're selling, and other manufacturers and importers too, that chimney cleaning must be an important aspect of our business."

After returning from Europe, Eva invited every chimney sweep she could find to a meeting at her offices. Most came. The time was right for chimney sweeps to make a comeback in America, they all agreed. From this meeting, the path was obvious. An association of Chimney Sweeps was needed. With her usual dynamic energy, Eva launched it.

By 1977, the Chimney Sweep Guild of America was well underway. Sweeps arrived in Portland to compare notes and learn the latest about brushes and new tools of their trade. Eva Horton was elected executive director for the guild.

"As a child, living in Oslo, Norway, I remember the slip of paper appearing regularly in the mailbox telling us that the chimney sweep was due the next day and to close our flues. Today, they make their rounds twice a year or more."

"With more people in the United States heating with wood stoves, it follows that regular chimney cleaning is important. You must remove the soot and the creosote that is deposited in chimneys during the natural process of burning wood," she explains.

Although the Chimney Sweep Guild is still in its early stages, members have realized that business potential is excellent. They charge from $35 to $55 for the first flue and slightly less for the second in the same house. Many report earnings of $400 to $600 per week. Many also are in the business of selling and servicing wood-burning stoves, both Jøtul and a wide range of others.

Having been aware of the need for chimney cleaning, Eva also saw an opportunity for her business. The sweeps in Europe had been at their unique work for years. They had perfected tools to do the job fast and effectively. Those too offered sales potential for her Kristia Associates.

Because many areas do not yet have a local chimney sweep, homeowners must do the job themselves when they use wood stoves regularly. After examining equipment that worked best in Europe, Eva began importing chimney cleaning brushes and equipment. She sells them through her dealer organization and through many other outlets, from supermarkets to hardware stores.

Because wood heating had been long neglected in

America, few people realized the need for chimney cleaning. Even with the members of the Chimney Sweep Guild working seven days a week, it would require an army of new recruits to keep pace with the demand for their services. Wood stoves today are being installed in hundreds of thousands of homes across the country.

Unlike buggy whips that came back to some extent for use in horse shows, chimney sweeps provide a more functional service. Dozens of enterprising men, and some women too, have donned top hat and tails to become sweeps. As one sweep noted at a recent gathering, "Chimney sweeps are really cleaning up." It's true. Eva is also helping them do it, profitably.

There are many ways to clean a chimney, but doing it right requires the proper equipment and know-how. Eva realized that few do-it-yourselfers would have the necessary expertise. A book on the subject was needed, she decided. So she wrote *The Chimney Brush, The Homeowners' Resource Book on the Art of Sweeping Chimneys.* It is selling well now through her dealers and in stores. It also features, promotes, and sells her new line of chimney brushes and says many kind words about her Jøtul stoves. Price is only $1 per copy. A revised, expanded edition is in the works, written by Eva, of course.

"Bumper stickers seem to have become an art form," she observes.

Effective bumper stickers were created and produced by her own advertising agency. They reflect her flair for powerful promotion. Each one carries a logo for her Jøtul stoves. One says simply, "Wood Heat—Yours For The Axing." Another says, "Burn Wood, Be A Son Of A Birch." Appealing to ecologists, one says, "Heat With Wood, They Never Spilled Logs At Santa Barbara."

Along Madison Avenue where the bright boys create advertising campaigns to turn customers on, Eva Horton may not be known. Nor did she take courses in the advertising arts. Nevertheless, the former housewife heads her own advertising agency that promotes the Jøtul stoves effectively.

Promotion has been a key to her success. Timing was perhaps the key factor initially. When motorists waited not so patiently in line to fuel their cars and home fuel prices climbed, Eva positioned herself strategically well. Other importers began establishing sales outlets for their stoves as American manufacturers began expanding their dealer networks.

Promotion was the key to staying on top and far ahead of the competition, Eva realized. Jøtul stoves still stand out in people's minds. They are one of the best types made, no doubt. But unless potential customers hear of them and learn about their virtues, sales don't materialize.

Today, behind her desk, on a plane or in a car, Eva Horton is intent on keeping sales stoked up. Her enthusiasm and energy are as boundless as the fires that fuel the zeal of missionaries. Her mission is a warmer world, well heated with wood stoves, her Jøtul stoves, of course.

8/Louis Kashey, Jr.— From Theater Arts and English Instructor to House Designer

His original goal was the theater. Studying psychology, English, theater arts at college, Lou was enthusiastically pursuing his objective. In the theater he saw opportunities to enjoy life thoroughly, express his creative skills, develop his talents, and direct actors and actresses in their performances. The lights of Broadway shone brightly before his eyes.

A graduate of Rutgers University with a Bachelors degree in psychology and a minor in theater arts, Lou was well on his way. His own performances had been reviewed favorably. The shows he had directed were well received. Plaudits were deserved. So was the applause.

He attended courses in Texas, worked on lighting, and did some directing at the Dallas Theater Center. He added to his experience at the Arena Stage in Washington, D.C. and the Cherry Lane Theater in Pennsylvania. Life on the wicked stage and behind it was moving merrily along. From dramatic productions to comedies, Lou was making his mark. Judging from the clippings, he was excellent in his chosen field.

Unfortunately, you may love what you are doing, but life in and around the theater isn't necessarily as financially rewarding as the audience on the other side of the footlights may believe it is. Still, Lou loved the theater. Greasepaint, they say, gets in your blood. A unique opportunity arose to be stage manager for the Arundel Opera Theater in Maine. In theater organizations away from Broadway, you have the opportunity to do many things and learn more that can enhance a career. Lou didn't exactly leap, but he headed north fast.

In the theater world, there is the real and the unreal. The real is what the audience believes they see, the actors and actresses moving through their roles, creating personalities and living those parts while the stage lights are lit. It can be exhilarating. The unreal is what is real. Once offstage, the actresses and actors become human beings again. Often they are lonely and insecure. The play's the thing, Shakespeare said. When the play is done, the life of the performer returns to what it was before the curtain rose and lights came on.

Few outside the theatrical world realize how different it can be after the curtain falls.

Lou has a large measure of idealist and dreamer in him. He enjoys the world and wishes, as many like him do, that it could be better. In the theater, surrounded by talented people, he began to discover that even there the difference between real and unreal, including the people, was not what it could or perhaps should be. Nevertheless, he continued his theater career.

"When I came to the Arundel Opera Company, it was widely known for its fine performances, both among audiences and in the theater world. It offered challenge and potential," he recalls.

At this point, however, he had seen the unseen behind

the scenes. Without the bright lights, the makeup, the costumes, and the crowd's applause, there was, he began to realize, a hypocrisy in the theater world.

"It's not quite real, not quite part of anything except the play at the time. Actors are people. They can be as petty as any other people, perhaps more so."

For several years, to supplement his income, Kashey became a substitute teacher. He also joined a small four-year college to teach theater arts, English, and humanities courses. In that position he could expand his proved creative talents, design sets, light the shows, bring talented performers to the college, and direct the plays as he wished. Through his efforts, Odetta, Edward Villela and others of their stature came to perform. He directed the first musical the college theater group had produced. He brought *Oh Dad, Poor Dad* to the community with a multimedia approach.

But the glow of the theater was dimming for him. He switched to teaching more, at the college level.

There was no flash of insight that made him retract his roots from the theater world. In fact, he still appreciates and attends good theater when he can. His switch to a new life and life-style was more transitional. Artistically inclined, he organized a business venture based on his theatrical background. With friends from the art world, Kashey decided that an art gallery that also added the dimension of musical performances might constitute an appealing combination. He opened his gallery in Ogunquit, a summer community widely noted for its artist's colony.

Artists from various parts of the country exhibited. Free concerts around his grand piano were offered. He realized that promotion and publicity are vital to a theater's success. Using the techniques he had gained from the theater, Kashey promoted well.

"I thought I knew what people were looking for, but I realized that they aren't even certain what they are looking for either. That summer was an important landmark. It was my first venture in business. Perhaps it wasn't exactly a financial success, but the lessons were of great value," he recalls.

Looking back to his experience at the Turnau Opera Company of Woodstock, Vermont, and the exceptional audience and public response to its performances, Kashey turned to another path. He hired the town hall in a small town and booked performers. They had the right credentials—they were top talent from the Metropolitan Opera Studio. Unfortunately the weather didn't cooperate.

"Those were the two foggiest nights of a foggy summer," he recalls. "That attempt to bring theater to a community, to continue a career allied to the theater, to opera, drama or the theater in general, was my last altruistic venture," he says sadly.

By 1974, Kashey had given up plans for a career in the theater. He isn't bitter or disappointed that the world he wanted wasn't what it seemed to be after the stage lights were turned out and the makeup was peeled away.

Kashey admits that the early 1970s were a transitional period. He wasn't groping or searching. Instead, he was refocusing his mind on new horizons that would enable him to harness his considerable creative and artistic abilities into a new arena.

He also admits easily, looking back, that "I spent my time in the trenches. I had to go one way or the other."

The question was, which way would best suit his artistic temperament and allow him greatest freedom to express his perception of life and achieve his own individual lifestyle.

In the interim, the energy crisis crunched. Kashey saw the future as an energy-conscious time, not just temporarily, but for the long pull through his lifetime and into the future beyond. Housing, he thought, had been restricted to a roof, walls, and inside partitions with little regard for the free flow of people and music and ideas. He opted for a shot at designing houses. He reasoned that his background as a set designer, his ability to visualize space and form and texture and flow of line would provide a sound background.

Without engineering training but with a sense of perseverance and a survival instinct, he and an associate designed a house. As it took shape, he focused on low costs, energy savings, and a more attractive design than the efficient but bleak mobile homes provided. He realized that to succeed, he must shape his future on the drawing board, create the building that combined both aesthetic values and low cost to compete for buyer dollars. It must be pleasing and affordable. It must compete in the low-cost housing market with mobile homes.

Reality of building material costs didn't always mesh with his plans and desires. Timing wasn't on his side in the low-cost building business.

"I liked and still do prefer space and freedom in a house," he notes. "Many people, today at last, have a greater feel for nature, for freedom and life's natural rhythms. I wanted to design homes that would express this to people and provide them with that sense of space and openness, a continuity of the outdoors and their dwelling. With building material costs today, it isn't a low-cost home I now design."

As he sought ways to capture the concepts he envisioned, a unique opportunity caught his imaginative eye. Silos are a landmark in rural areas where farmers store their silage and feed for livestock. There's an openness to them, a blend with nature, trees, and plants. Standing inside a silo, one has a feeling of space. Although it is enclosed, the sense of enclosure is nothing like the four walls of square or rectangular buildings, Kashey believes.

Since he likes openness in the world around him, he visualized homes in the round. When ideas strike, you must move with them. That has been the mark of creative people.

The Unadilla Silo Company at that time was offering round houses based on their silo technology. The match was made. Kashey moved into the round world of round houses as an agent for the company.

Today he operates a company called, appropriately,

the Maine Round House. He designs homes around the principle of the silo. His own home is nearing completion. An airiness and loftiness of soaring space is evident throughout the home.

He quips that no matter how much energy you have yourself, you still need alternate energy sources to stay warm in winter. Building houses isn't exactly winter work. Designing them is. But cash flow is important all year round.

Kashey doesn't think vertically like most people. Nor does he necessarily think around in circles. He tends to think laterally, exploring avenues that others have passed by. Often great ideas are missed because they are too simple or too obvious. People tend to make things complicated for themselves, more complicated than they need to be. Kashey doesn't.

He combined the best of things around him—his round house, the trees and woods surrounding it—and solved his energy needs. He became one of the first retail outlets for the famed Jøtul wood-burning stoves. Today he has a hot business going with them too.

As he was considering energy needs, insulation, and other factors to blend homes with people into the environment, Kashey realized there were options. There was growing interest in wind power, solar energy heaters, and other alternatives. In the wooded areas of America, especially New England, wood abounds.

"The woods are full of trees," he observes with a wry smile. "Sometimes it takes a while to see the trees for the forest."

Time has proved Kashey correct. Wood stoves have become a major factor in the rush to find alternate energy sources as fuel bills pile higher. Hundreds of thousands of wood stoves are being sold each year across the country. They fit ideally into his house designs. Without restrictive walls, partitions, and needless compartments within a round house, wood stoves provide a natural complement.

They heat space well. Heat rises. By designing houses that have free flow of air and heat, Kashey has combined the attributes of both his homes and a logical alternate heating system.

His Jøtul stoves are imported from Norway by Kristia Associates.

Kashey met Eva Horton when she first launched her enterprise. They became friends. Today he is one of the larger Jøtul dealers in New England. His self-taught expertise in house design and his feel for natural surroundings led him naturally into designing and installing chimneys, fireplaces, wood stoves, and home heating alternatives.

"Wood stoves are here. But for most people, they are an alternate heating system. Many people buy them and use them as such or as a backup system. Some may use them as a primary source, but that will depend, in time, on availability of low-cost wood as a fuel," he observes.

Wood stove sales have continued climbing for Kashey and hundreds of other retail dealers who foresaw them as a major alternate home heating. For him, the stoves provide the perfect complement to his home design and building business. They provide the week-by-week cash flow and working capital. Even in the summer season, when people wouldn't necessarily be thinking of winter heating problems, he sells stoves at his showroom and office. Tourists from the entire eastern coast and Canada flock to the New England seashore in summer. Many order stoves to be shipped back to their homes when vacation ends.

Many people also stop to study Kashey's round house plan. His own home is a showplace prototype. Even contractors have visited to probe the potentials for construction in their home areas.

Kashey expects to design, sell and supervise construction of five to ten homes per year. Although he had originally planned to design low-cost homes, there isn't a sufficiently strong market for what some consider the offbeat-looking house. Many people don't have the ability to visualize what a silo home can be. And with the rising price of materials, it just isn't possible to design and create these homes and still keep costs competitive with mobile homes or small cottages, Kashey believes. But he sees them as a new trend in the energy-conserving era.

Despite that switch in his plans and the necessary adjustment in his thinking, Kashey is breaking new ground in home design and wood-stove applications. He's convinced as much by customer acceptance as by his own belief that wood stoves will become as commonplace in the future as kitchen stoves.

He also points out that round houses have advantages in fuel cost reduction. Round houses have an important wind dispersal factor. There isn't the same cold north wall that chills the inside of a conventional house, he explains. Instead, wind moves around the home.

Round houses also collect light all around. By proper placing of windows you can capture passive solar heat. Then, with proper insulation and closures for windows at night, you can hold the accumulated heat in the building.

Although ceilings may seem to soar in the silo portions of Kashey's appealing round house, wood stoves and adequate insulation make it snug in the most frigid weather. His basic heating is electric. However, calculations he has done in conjunction with building engineers point to low total heating costs, well under half the cost of conventional heating. Wood stoves are the key. Many people agree. They are buying stoves as fast as shipments arrive.

"I am in the business to sell stoves, and houses, of course," he readily admits. "But if you aren't accurate, you lose customers. People today are consumer oriented. They want facts and figures. That's why I handle only the type of stoves that will fulfill customer expectations. I intend to be in business for a long time. Repeat business, word of mouth, will be the key to keeping customers coming through my door."

The Jøtul stoves, imported from Norway, have a unique feature. Baffle systems inside the cast-iron stoves help burn the volatile gases that would otherwise rise up a typical fireplace chimney. Those gases are a source of heat too. In addition, the air-tight construction of these Norwegian stoves is important. Wood burns slowly from front to back. Heat is more uniform. This controlled burning cuts down the amount of wood needed compared to conventional stoves or Franklin fireplaces.

At the round house in Kennebunkport, Maine, Kashey displays the full line of Jøtul stoves, from the small ones that take fifteen-inch logs and heat a good-size room, to the large models that can warm half a house well. He also features other stoves and a variety of accessories, from cleaning brushes to tools.

Proper installation is important with wood stoves, he cautions. They should be placed away from combustible walls. Chimneys should be carefully installed to provide proper draft. If old chimneys are used for wood stoves, they should be checked, repaired if necessary, and cleaned periodically. His firm provides design and installation services for all customers. A local chimney sweep is recommended for cleaning.

Whatever heating system a person adopts, adequate and proper insulation is the first vital step, Kashey believes. He and other people in construction underline the word *proper* when speaking of insulation. It is the least expensive, but has been proved the most important step in saving energy in home heating. Walls should be insulated, window frames caulked, ceilings capped with extra-thick insulation. Storm windows or special energy-saver windows can be utilized in new home construction. Insulated draperies and shades can be hung to keep the accumulated heat in at night.

Venting also is important to permit proper air flow that avoids trapping moisture inside walls, which can lead to rotting wood and frames. There's much to learn and teach, Kashey points out. He feels we are all entering an era that will last our lifetimes. Energy saving, despite anyone's belief that oil or gas prices may be artificially inflated, is necessary today. It will be even more important in the future.

"Wood stoves work well, efficiently and effectively," he emphasizes. "However," he explains his belief, based on common sense, logic, and an understanding of the laws of supply and demand, "wood stoves are only as valuable to save fuel costs as a reasonably priced wood supply. They will be part of the scene in practically every home in rural America where wood supplies are available in the next decade. But if wood is in short supply, prices will climb naturally and make wood just an alternate to oil while costs will tend to equalize." He urges all customers to line up their wood supply now. He recommends storing several years' supply if possible, and contracting or otherwise arranging to have adequate hardwood cut and delivered.

Fortunately, wood grows on trees. Wood today and tomorrow can be money saved. From separate interviews with wood stove customers, it can be seen that many are taking the long look ahead. They are indeed lining up supplies. Some are investing in vacation acreage to have supplies for the future. American ingenuity and resilience seem to be alive and well today.

Looking at his own future in his new life and career, Louis Kashey is planting his roots firmly and well. He's space oriented in housing design and living. He's gauging his future with a seasoned and sharp eye for business. His future in his new life-style will include music and theater, observing and enjoying in his round house world. No doubt the crackle of logs burning in his own and the many wood stoves he sells will warm his heart and keep his home fire burning brightly. He's a new pioneer.

In 1978, Kashey sold his wood stove business in order to concentrate on his home-designing business. He still, however, warms himself with wood stoves in his roundhouse home.

9/Oscar Adolph—From Advertising Executive To Farmer

Madison Avenue's advertising row stretches for twenty blocks in the Big Apple. Some advertising agencies may list addresses off the street, but basically, Madison Avenue is the world of the tricky phrase, the eye-blink package, the Brooks Brothers suit, and the media mix that drive consumers to the store to buy and buy again.

Mind manipulation isn't new. It dates to ancient times when serfs bowed reverently to their lords. It's been called many things. It's creative enterprise; it also is a black art, some believe.

Oscar Adolph spent fifteen years along Mad Ave. They were especially sweet financially. Few careers offer dollar rewards to the brash and the bold so young. Salaries of $20,000 to $50,000 are not uncommon if you can capture the public's attention with a jingle, a phrase, a thirty-second TV message.

"It's exciting, it's challenging, it's fun, it's the big-buck world," Adolph says. "There's exhilaration in the fact that a million people buy a toilet paper because you told them it is soft and easy on their budget. When you can convince ten million more to swill a mouthwash, suds their armpits, become sex symbols with a six-dollar bottle of what you sell, that's a score, no doubt about it.

"Sure, there's truth in advertising. Today, self-appointed watchdogs and government officials keep watch through the night."

But on Madison Avenue, Diogenes wouldn't do too well. Someone would probably sell his candle for twice what it was worth.

Adolph, despite bittersweet memories, doesn't regret his years as a highly paid product tout. He actually relishes his contributions to his former clients' sales success. He has awards to prove his work's worth and a bank account to back up those certificates as well.

Why, if his world was greener each year than most people's in ten years, did he pull up his profitable roots? It's a fair question.

"It was time to stop conning myself," he says simply, without a blink or blush or apology. "I was good at the ad game. It fascinated me. The expense accounts were enough to live on deliciously. The agency life was stimulating—new ideas, creative people, action morning, noon, night, weekends.

"Actually, I was bored. I had done it all. And I knew I could keep doing it. But one day, catching the special out of Greenwich, I saw a tree. The leaves had turned brown and were falling to the ground. I stopped and picked up a handful of leaves. They were dry, so I crumpled them in my hand and they fell apart.

"I caught the train to Grand Central, rode the usual subway uptown, climbed the same stairs to Madison Avenue, saw the same numbers runner in the lobby, opened the same office door, sat in the same genuine leather executive swivel chair.

"I reached in my pocket, took out the crumpled oak tree leaves and spread them on my desk. There was the usual mail, client phone call memos, appointment book listing the day's schedule for TV shooting, art and creative meetings.

"As everyone on the avenue knows, you don't drink dry Beefeaters martinis until lunch. But instead of coffee I had my secretary make a martini for me, twist the lemon peel just so, and hold my calls.

"It was a frightening feeling, sitting there, knowing I had it made; realizing in a few more years I would have more money invested in CDA, funds, stocks, bonds, really have it made to take it easy. And I looked at the dry leaves again. First thing in my head was an idea for a TV commercial, dry leaves, dry hair, our client's shampoo with conditioner could solve the problem. We could do a storyboard in a week, screen the models, do the commercial on location and pick up extra money for out-of-town expenses.

"The second idea followed from the first: tie up old man nature, the natural ingredients in the shampoo, pitch to the environment and back to earth when you use this shampoo. Those thoughts ran about three minutes. I could have sold the idea to the client, built a whole new campaign, beat the bastard down the hall, who also worked on the account, to the next level up the agency ladder.

"What really hit me was that I hadn't noticed the leaves turn color on the trees. Sitting there, looking at those old crumpled leaves, my head started down the same path again. I visualized green leaves, fresh and soft and mellow, turning colors and finally brown. I saw the TV commercials take form . . . the country and a beautiful model . . . not realizing she was getting old and her hair needed our shampoo to keep its youth. That's when I knew I had to quit. Even the perfect dry martini tasted crumpled and dead."

Adolph recalls that he rearranged the crumbled leaves for about an hour, even trying to piece them back into a leaf.

He thought he might be having a nervous breakdown when he looked up and realized his secretary was in the doorway, staring at him. He thought about cornfields in Iowa years back, and the smell of the hogs and the tours of client plants to see their products made, and the weeks watching shoppers buy products on supermarket shelves.

"I went home at noon and walked around town. I looked at cars: Lincolns, Cadillacs, Mercedes at the station. I walked past hundred- and two-hundred-thousand-dollar homes. My wife was out for the day, so I sat on the patio and watched the grass grow."

Decision making was easy for Oscar Adolph. He made decisions every day. On his decisions rode millions of dollars every year, many millions. He could spend a million dollars with a phone call to a client and to a TV network to sponsor a top-rated network TV show.

It took him a week to make the final move, his memo of resignation. During the week, he looked at flowers, trees, grass, stars, and people. Mainly he remembers people. He remembers too how they looked back at him. He recalls saying hello to people he didn't know on the street, in New York, in the subway and in the elevator.

The clincher was a simple thing; just one person in an elevator. He freely admits he overreacted to that phrase at the time. But he attributes that one line to the final decision that led to his new life today.

"I was standing in the elevator heading to my lofty executive floor. A friend, another account executive, came in and stood in the front. He pushed the button for his floor . . . then he jabbed 'Door Close' several times, five, I think. I said, 'Hi, how are you today?'

"He turned on me and so help me, I'll never forget it, he said, 'What the hell do you really care!' He got off, turned down the hall and that's the last time I ever saw him. But I'm still grateful to him. I went to my office, took out the resignation letter I had written, and tore it up. In its place I typed out four words on a 3×5 file card, put it in my pocket and called the president of the agency.

"He talked first. The usual about hot new ideas, creativity, how well I was handling my accounts. That lasted five minutes. The next five were about new ideas, new campaigns, new business proposals I should handle. I could see myself in that executive chair, doing the same thing, at five times my present salary. So I handed him my file card and stood up. He read it and laughed.

"I laughed too. All I said was thanks, but I meant it. We shook hands. He said he knew I was tired and needed a week off. I said, thanks anyway, and left. You know, I never hear from any of the top people there, but I guess I asked for that."

Oscar Adolph and family now farm. He never did before. City boys and city girls don't really know how. But he and she and their children do.

For example, friends in Greenwich, Darien, and along Madison Avenue were at first horrified. When they heard he had fled to a farm, they were amused. Some were concerned, of course, but not the ones he had thought might be. The concerned ones were primarily far below his status. They assumed he had broken down. They offered to help. A few even came over to his house to talk and listen.

"Those, we still see periodically. They even come to Vermont on vacation, buy eggs, fruit, and vegetables from us.

"Farming is more than a way to live. It is a way of life, despite what the magazines say about the need for mass production, large acreage, efficient production," Adolph believes. True, he had a bigger bank account than most. It's down to a low level today.

But the bees buzz in his orchard and people buy his honey; the apples and pears and berries bring in some money. The bacon is better now than the bacon he ate when he killed and butchered his first pig. A few crossed cattle graze in a pasture along a brook. Daisies and black-eyed Susans bloom near the old Cape Cod style house where he and his family live.

For a city boy, Adolph can describe his land better

than someone born to the farm. By commercial standards, it will never support a family. It is, judging from the county extension agent's analysis, barely self-sustaining, but to Oscar Adolph, it is home.

He drives a battered Ford pickup. His wife has an aging Dodge sedan that should last a few more years. A John Deere tractor, circa whatever era, still mows hay and with its power take-off belt connected to an antique buzz saw, cuts fireplace wood.

Is he content?

"In my own way, yes."

Is his wife?

"I think so, but you can ask her. She says she is and I really think so."

What about the kids?

"They fish, hunt, help around the place. They play ball on the school team; get respectable grades too."

Why?

"If you must ask, you wouldn't understand my answer anyway."

Adolph has praise for his neighbors, high praise. When he first moved to the run-down farm, neighbors considered him a rich, spoiled city guy, he says. The more he messed up and floundered, the more he amused them.

When his well went dry and his first beef animal died, people offered help. When scab infected his apples, a neighbor drove a sprayer down the road to help stop the problem and save his crop.

"People are pretty basic here. They leave you alone, but when they realize you're in trouble, they stop by to help. If you admit you are stupid, they really come to your rescue. In two years, I'm not a real farmer yet, and may never be. But we haven't starved and we've made a lot of good friends.

"The county agricultural agent helped a lot too. He gave us advice on fertilizing this farm, which pigs to raise, how to keep animals healthy, which pesticides to use and when. With people like him, the home economics agent to help us can and preserve food, and lots of reading in books, we'll be okay.

"By the way," Adolph added as an afterthought, "try this maple syrup on your pancakes. It's sweetest, from the sugar maples that have the brightest color in the fall."

10/Donna Sabaka—
From Housewife to Book Illustrator

Alan Sabaka—
From Dry Cleaner to Helicopter Pilot

Ashland, Ohio, is a pleasant town. Her parents still live there along with other members of her family. When high school days were gone, she dutifully headed on to college at Bowling Green State University, also in her native Ohio. College, despite the courses she enjoyed in art, wasn't all that exciting. One man did excite her, but he flew off into military service soon after they had met.

Rather than continue studies that didn't turn her on, Donna Sabaka opted for more challenge in the real world outside college doors. She attended some art courses in Cleveland, but Cleveland isn't exactly an artist's mecca either. Breezes blowing from the Windy City drifted across Ohio. A friend had moved there earlier and her letters held promise of fame and fortune in Chicago. There was action there, lots of it. Opportunities were there. You could make it big in Chicago, the letters implied. Donna packed up and moved. Fame and fortune were just over the horizon. On the shore of Lake Michigan, her ship would come in.

"I was raised with all the usual midwestern proprieties," she explains. "And I had the normal expectations of any young person . . . dreaming of the good life in the big city. My definition of the good life and the definition other people had in the big city didn't quite mesh."

During her first year, Donna learned other definitions. She enjoyed free lunches, dinners, and offers of fame and fortune enough to satisfy anyone. Chicago offered give and take if you wished to give and take.

She learned that a studio coach in an art studio is similar to a casting coach in the theatrical world. She learned that being a natural model had a far different meaning from what she at first had assumed. Declining invitations and offers, she realized, soon led to declining fortunes in the art world.

"When an artist says he would like to 'do you,' it doesn't necessarily mean paint you. When you get an offer to express yourself, that doesn't usually mean on canvas, either," she adds. Ashland, Ohio, began to look better.

More disappointed than disillusioned, but much wiser in the ways of the world, she headed home. "An artist may have to sacrifice a lot of things to be an artist, but there are lots of things I didn't feel like sacrificing," she adds.

Her brushes, easel, canvases, drawing board, and other art supplies spent the next few years in an attic trunk.

"When someone asks whether you want to get into the action, they usually aren't talking about art either," she recalls. "And," she adds, "I wasn't ready for or interested in that much action."

Her return to her hometown wasn't really a retreat. She became engaged, married, and when her husband flew off to Vietnam to pilot helicopters, she settled in to become the soul of propriety, a happy housewife in Ohio. It was the cozy, comfortable nest that many her age preferred.

"Several thousand washloads later, I realized that

housewifing wasn't really what I wanted to do," Donna emphasizes. "When Al returned from Vietnam, we spent a lot of time talking, thinking, and debating with ourselves what it really was we wanted to do. One thing we both knew, we wanted to get out of the role or rut we were putting ourselves in. Others were settling into their routine, but that wasn't for us."

Like other new pioneers, the Sabakas had family roots in their communities. Alan Sabaka could have joined his father in the family dry cleaning business. He had worked in it up to the time he flew off to Nam.

Like other new pioneers, they decided to uproot themselves completely. It seemed logical, they recall. When you can't decide what you want to do, but at least know what you don't want to do, you're about half way to becoming a new pioneer.

They had honeymooned by the ocean in New England. Both liked the sea. Both felt an urge to transplant themselves to a completely different life and life-style. What it would be, they couldn't define, but they had exuberance and youth on their side.

Six years ago, the Sabakas packed up and headed off to Maine. They had no jobs or even faint promises of jobs.

"We had $600 in our savings account, an old car, and a one-and-a-half-year-old daughter," Donna recalls. "I was pregnant. That would be four mouths to feed and more loads of washing to do, but I guess we felt more like homesteaders."

The Homestead was a somewhat drafty house on quaintly named Log Cabin Road, in the woods of coastal Maine. Homesteading also was jobs for both of them in an electrical product manufacturing plant. They took turns working different shifts so one would be home with their young daughter. Donna worked on the assembly line until three weeks before their son was born.

Winter winds blow cold on the coast of Maine. Snow drifts high. At night, drifts often have blown back across the state road to stall a car for hours until you shovel your way through. The wind chill factor drops the degree level to far below zero. It numbs your bones.

There had to be a better way, the Sabakas knew. Since Alan had been a dry cleaner before cutting out to be on his own, he explored a related business idea. Winter snow must be plowed. Sand and salt on roads and streets are tracked into homes, motels, hotels, restaurants. Carpet cleaning could be salable. He bought a machine and a truck. Atlantic Steamway Cleaning was in business.

"It was," Alan recalls, "a way to keep wolves from the door, meat on the table, and buy time to find our way here in the north woods."

Business grew. His quality work attracted more customers. He contracted with motels and hotels, banks and restaurants. Their income grew, but the hours did too.

"When you are in a business like this, you work when the customers call. That's at night mostly, in the oddest hours. You can't steam-clean carpets when people are eating dinner or bankers are banking," Sabaka explains. "Anyone that says you are lucky to be on your own, so you can set your own hours, take all the time off you want, is living in a fantasy world. You are more bound by your customers than if you worked in a factory nine to five."

He could have gone back to steady, routine work, That would have given him "normal" hours to live a "normal life," be with his family more, have the security of fringe benefits and a company retirement plan.

Sabaka's pioneer blood wouldn't allow that. As pioneers had plodded their way west, fought the elements and their neighbors at times, Sabaka fought to keep his freedom. He kept it and his options too. He recalls cleaning carpets between 2:00 and 5:00 A.M. with only the hum of his equipment to break the monotony. On the job and off, he let his mind fly to those better ways he and his wife discussed, when they could match their schedules to be together.

Having been an instructor pilot in the army, teaching the basics and fine points of helicopters, Sabaka enjoyed flying. He didn't necessarily enjoy being under the thumb of senior officers with their doctrinaire minds, "But even in the military, when you're flying, you have a feeling of independence until you report back to base," he points out. Freedom, in his mind, was somehow connected with the sky and flying.

Donna, meantime, washed more thousands of loads of clothes. Between washloads and meal preparation, dishwashing and other dutiful duties, she sketched. Nature and the things that grew and flew were her favorite subjects.

Today, Al Sabaka flies again. His wife put wings to her dreams too. She is now a book illustrator and cartoonist and is closing in fast on her goal—to be an artist on her own.

"There was a funny story years back about house husbands in Sweden," she recalls. "We both laughed about it because it was treated like big news. We didn't have defined roles and hadn't since we came to Maine. If I was painting or drawing, Al would cook the meal and do the dishes. If he needed help to clean a bank's board room, I could substitute on that job as well as any helper he had hired."

The longing for personal freedom and independence was a mark of the original pioneers. They had guts that seem to have disappeared from the population alive today. The Sabakas were not related to those early American pioneers. They did, however, have the perseverance and persistence of homesteaders.

Alan has completed plans to put his flying venture into the air. With friends who also have the new pioneering spirit, he has spent endless days meeting with bank officials, the Small Business Administration, investors, and aircraft manufacturers.

His idea wouldn't fly, he had been told many times. The world is filled with negative-minded people. Fortunately, there are some farsighted ones who still look ahead to new horizons. They agreed with him that his new horizon was in the sky.

Sabaka will be flying the skies of New England. His courier service, by helicopter and light plane, will speed documents from bank to bank. He'll fly traffic studies. He'll carry sportsmen on fishing expeditions to lakes that can't be reached by roads or even by logging trail. He'll fill the needs of harried executives to be in places faster than ground-bound transportation could get them there. He'll also enjoy his own personal freedom in the air and around the state he rerooted himself into.

Donna didn't let her dream die either. A mutual acquantance mentioned to an author that she was talented in art. They met. The timing was right. He needed artwork done; she wanted to do it.

Her first book-illustrating assignment was slightly less than terrifying, she recalls. "I'd done art that pleased me, but never anything commercial. My portfolio, if that's what it could be called, was a pile of drawings, sketches, a mess of other things I had started and not quite had time to finish."

Her strokes were bold. Her feel for translating an author's idea was firm. Although she was as undisciplined as many artists that she knew, the author was persistent.

"He was often on the doorstep when the sun came up, on the phone a few times each day and pestering me on Sunday afternoons as well," she says. "At first, it didn't seem quite real. You don't become a book illustrator or an artist for syndicated columns sitting in a kitchen in the woods." But she did. Her illustrations first appeared in a Fawcett paperback. The next set, with her own "Illustrated By," were in a Doubleday hardcover.

Her sharp, clear, bold strokes next illustrated nationally syndicated columns for a major news feature service. Two other books were launched.

Watching as her children grew, Donna used them as models. She asked them to move a thousand different ways to achieve the look she wanted as she drew hands, feet, and faces.

The next book with her name in print appeared last spring, profusely illustrated with her precisely executed line drawings. *The Big Fun to Grow Book*, a handsome hardcover from another New York publisher, carried her name on the cover. Other publishers called her author friend to ask about her availability.

"She's just a housewife," an indignant New York editor pouted. "How can she do the quality work we need?" The author insisted. A budget was set. She illustrated again and again and again.

Her illustrations will be featured in a landscaping book due to be published soon. An annual almanac for another prestigious publisher in New York includes fifty Sabaka drawings. More children's book assignments were fulfilled. Two more books are being completed now. Six more are in the talking stage.

As yet, she has never met an editor or art director for whom she illustrated a book. "I haven't even talked with one by phone," she laughs. "But with the Xerox samples of my work, they don't even question whether a housewife in the Maine woods can do what they require."

The World Beneath Your Feet, another children's book, was published in 1977. The descriptions and illustrations of nature's mysterious underground, of the creatures large and small that live where most people never look already is winning critical acclaim. Her art style has improved with every book, editors in New York and Boston marvel. "It's a clean, refreshing style, no gunk and garbage to it," one remarked.

During dinner one evening, the telephone rang insistently. A retired college professor with a flair for public speaking had heard about her. He too had moved north and was living in a nearby town. "Do you do cartoons?" he asked.

That was one art area she hadn't explored. But out on

the new frontier you never say no, especially when dollars are involved. She admitted to having had a long-buttoned-up desire to do cartoons. They met.

Her clean, refreshing style worked its miracle again. Not only did she capture his ideas in her cartoons, she captured the likeness of both the retired college president and his wife. The new cartoon series, along with his periodic columns, now appear in local newspapers. In time they expect to develop their own self-syndicated strip with the series.

Donna has expanded her areas of influence in art. Standing at an old grist mill, she intently transfers her visual sensations to canvas. Occasionally she works in oil or pastels, but mostly in watercolors. Donna paints for fun. And, she adds, she paints for practice.

"Art is like music. You can't perform well with a piano or a flute without hours of practice. You must do the same with a brush, pen and ink or whatever medium you use. Besides being outdoors at the beach while the children are enjoying the surf, I can catch a lobster boat on canvas, or a bunch of dune grass or the Goat Island lighthouse," she says.

Commercially Donna Sabaka is building a reputation too. She had pen-and-inked for local businesses. Her designs for their menus, postcards, and advertising reflect the distinctive style or decor of each business.

"I still, of course, look at those loads of washing to do, and meals to cook, and all the other housewifely things that are necessary, but I don't feel like a housewife," she explains. "By drawing, or illustrating or painting, I have freedom; a chance to be myself and express what I think and feel."

Next step ahead is the world of art shows. She has been asked to assemble a collection of her works, from simple pen drawings to watercolors. Other artists have offered encouragement. A cross-section representation of area artists draws crowds, they assure her. Art shows, whether in individual galleries or in shopping malls, are crowd pleasers. Crowds attract crowds. If one style or picture doesn't appeal to one individual, there are hundreds more that stop and shop.

Winters are still long and harsh along the Maine coast. With her husband flying off again, this time on his own long-anticipated adventure in private enterprise, Donna is planning for her own creative career. There will be, she intends, art shows, advertising posters, book illustrations, even mechanical layouts and simple commercial art pasteups and assignments. Diversity is bankable.

"You may not like every piece of art you do, but even pioneers had to eat," she smiles.

Alan and Donna Sabaka both have no thoughts of returning to the routine they left far behind. They both put wings to their dreams. Together, they know they can make their dreams fly.

11/Allan Armstrong—From Army Officer to Carnivorous Plant Grower

Belly down, crawling through a swamp on the Carolina coast some eighteen years ago, a young army lieutenant directed his platoon to slither stealthily. Their objective for the training maneuver was a machine gun emplacement less than half a mile away. Observers were grading the exercise and the young lieutenant was concentrating intensely. He planned to make a career of the army as a regular officer after having graduated as an honor student from college. As a cadet colonel and commandant of the ROTC brigade at college, he was on his way to a bright future in the military.

It was that, he thought as he lay on the oozing ground, or back to the family's poultry farm in New Jersey. His family also had a dairy farm and a fruit-growing operation. Their roots were deep in the soil of the Garden State.

Suddenly a gaunt civilian, ruddy faced with two days' stubble on his chin, came roaring across the swamp.

"Git your goddamn Yankee soldiers off my land. You're killin' my crops," the old boy bellowed and added goddamn Yankee again for good measure.

The lieutenant rolled fast, came to a firing position and within minutes had two soldiers guarding their civilian prisoner. Brilliant move, he thought. Picked up a civilian informer for interrogation. Despite the old man's curses and struggles, they loaded him into the camouflaged jeep that was concealed at the edge of the swamp to move him to battalion headquarters for questioning.

"I'll see you court-martialed. You're trespassing on my land, ruining my plants, goddamn Yankees," their prisoner howled.

An older, seasoned sergeant tapped the eager young lieutenant on the arm.

"Sir, I checked the compass reading and the map. I think we really should be about a mile away from here. This may really be his land," the sergeant pointed out. Only a trace of a smirk crossed his face.

Trying to keep his cool, the lieutenant decided to question his prisoner again. He asked him what type of plants the troops in the platoon were ruining in a swamp.

"Carnivorous plants," the old boy bellowed. "You goddamn soldiers are crushing them."

"Okay, where are they?" the lieutenant asked. Their prisoner walked over to the bog and knelt down. "There, and there and there . . . all over this swamp."

An hour later, after apologies to the landowner and admitting to being a jackass of a Yankee, the lieutenant was stalking the machine-gun nest where it was really located, a mile away. But he had learned that there really is a strange world of carnivorous plants that lie hidden in swamps all along the Atlantic coastal plain.

Two weeks later, on a three-day pass, the lieutenant was back at the swamp to apologize again, present a large bottle of 100-proof bourbon to the landowner, and make peace. They talked for hours and walked miles of swamp land.

Today, eighteen years later, that former army officer sells the same plants he and his platoon were crushing into the soggy ground. He sells them worldwide by mail order, to schools, students, and plant enthusiasts. Looking back, Allan Armstrong recalls that encounter as one of the stupidest he had ever had, and perhaps the luckiest. It turned his career around. Within six months he had completed his active army duty and returned to civilian life.

"The next stupidest thing was telling my father that I planned to forget about poultry farming and dairy and fruit growing and concentrate on starting a carnivorous plant business.

"Pop just shook his head and asked how I really planned to make a living doing something like that. Then he bet me five dollars that I couldn't. So I put up five dollars and we agreed to set up a business with ten dollars of total capital. Meanwhile, I had thirty days of terminal leave from the army, so that gave me some money to live on."

With a wife and a year-old son to support, his decision was not exactly based on sound business judgment. But thirty days could prove out an idea. After all, old Bill in North Carolina had made a living raising and selling these botanical oddities just in the southeastern part of the United States. If more people lived in the northeastern area, it seemed logical that there would be buyers. Besides, he figured, there was the crackle berry business to pursue.

Taking chances on things from weather to insects is a normal part of a farmer's life. True, Armstrong recalls, starting a business with ten dollars was taking a long leap into space, but all he could lose was the bet and the money.

The first step in transplanting himself from the farm to the hoped-for new career in the wicked world of carnivorous plants was keeping everything secret. Who needs relatives looking at you funny every day?

The second step was assembling a list of several hundred names of garden centers, schools, and florist shops from dozens of telephone directories.

"I had had several long talks in person and by phone

with old Bill in North Carolina. He had agreed that for a Yankee I wasn't really that bad, just young and still a bit wet behind the ears. So he agreed to let me try selling these plants in New Jersey and the Northeast. If I could build up sales, he proposed to work out a long-term agreement to supply me with the plants that he grew."

The third step was typing a sales letter and printing it with pictures of the strange, insect-eating plants. It was neatly folded with an order form and self-addressed envelope and mailed to the 300 names assembled from the telephone directories. That used up the entire ten dollars of working capital.

The first week, mails being what they are, no replies came in. The second week, one order for fifteen dollars worth of plants arrived. After the cost of plants, box and postage, the new venture still showed a loss.

The third week, two calls came in. One was a reminder from the army that only two weeks were left to apply for a new assignment and a career with the regular army. The other was from a discount store in Trenton, New Jersey. It was from the owner.

"I remember that call and the meeting next morning vividly. It really turned the tide in my mind, which was still sloshing around with all sorts of worries at that point," Armstrong says.

"He asked if these plants really attracted, caught and ate insects. I assured him they did and would be glad to prove it the next day. We agreed to meet at 8:30 before his store opened.

"I packed up several of the most unusual plants, the Venus Fly Traps and Sundews, that were growing in glass brandy snifters. These plants require high humidity to give off their proper insect-luring aromas and then have the strength in their cells to catch the insect meals they need.

"We talked about the plants and how they worked for a half hour. Then he put me and the plants to the test. He simply said, 'Let's see them catch something.' So I took several flies from a jar and shook them into the large brandy snifter with the plants. They buzzed around and crawled on the side of the glass. Several flew out.

"The store owner watched without saying anything. Finally he said, 'Allan, if that thing catches a fly I'll give you an order for $1,000, but the plant only has another five minutes to do it.'

"We waited. Another fly crawled across the outer edge of the Venus Fly Trap plant and left. Then one of the few remaining flies landed, sniffed, and crept inside the cocked trap. It touched the first trigger hair and then brushed its wing against the second. That's what is needed to trigger the trap, and it did. The trap snapped, the cilia or fingers on the leaves clutched, and the fly was caught. Damn, did I breathe easier."

Good as his word, the store owner reached into his desk, wrote out a check for $1,000, and agreed to sign it when a supply of plants was delivered to the New Jersey State Fair in Trenton in two weeks.

The only problem was simple to solve. He wanted 500 live flies too. One afternoon in a dairy barn was enough to accumulate several hundred plump flies in large mason jars. These were systematically fed into a gigantic glass terrarium at the fair, a few every hour, under the sign, "Carnivorous Plants—Feeding Time Every Hour."

Students, plant enthusiasts, teachers, the curious lined up to watch Fly Traps snap and Sundews wrap sticky tentacles around their insect prey. The hundreds of plants were sold in two days.

"That event, weird as it was, did launch my new career as keeper and cultivator of carnivorous plants," Armstrong says with a smile. "Fact is, that first major customer now operates greenhouses in central New Jersey and continues to order bulbs, roots, and plants every year."

This particular transplanting from army or poultry farm to carnivorous plants may not seem as abrupt an uprooting as those of others who have opted for different life-styles. But the world of carnivorous plants that Armstrong cultivated during the past eighteen years and pursues today is a fascinating one.

Through those years of traveling the country and around the world in search of botanical wonders, meeting customers and building worldwide sales, the change of life-style has taken strange turns. Despite increases in postage and mailing costs, labor problems and general inflation, the wicked world of carnivorous plants has actually been a wonderland of reasonable profit and unusual customers.

"From that first sale in New Jersey, I've really built this offbeat business on oddball promotions. People are naturally curious. They want to see the unusual, learn about it, and tell their friends stories about their odd plants."

From the Venus Fly Traps and Sundews he expanded into other fascinating carnivorous plants. Within a year or two he had arranged to obtain other plants with similar habits from people in other parts of the country and the world. Over the years, he contracted to have plants grown in Oregon, Florida, Alabama, and imported from Europe as well. The more articles appeared about these plants which he raised, the more letters came in from Asia, Africa, Canada, Europe, even from islands in the Indian Ocean.

Perhaps the key to the initial and continued success of what came to be Armstrong Associates, Inc. and its Plant Oddities division was the realization that odd plants made news. If a dog bites a person, that's to be expected. But, when a person bites a dog, that's news. It follows that plants eating animals and insects instead of the reverse can generate news and publicity.

One of the first activities of the fledgling plant oddities business was taking photographs of the strange plants. They were fed flies, moths, mosquitoes, gnats, and even a grasshopper to eat. As they grasped their meals, a photographer clicked away. Photos were used in the initial advertising and news releases.

Publicity is a marketing tool, Armstrong believes. Many newspapers and magazines are looking for interesting stories, something to catch the eye and capture reader attention. The close-up photographs of hungry carnivorous plants devouring a butterfly hit the headlines. The story was brief. It said simply, "Hungry Plants Eat Live Insects," with a short explanation and the name and address of where such plants could be obtained, plus the price.

Dozens of newspapers ran the story. So did a few mass circulation magazines. Checks and orders poured in. The merry tune the first full year in business was just over $8,000 in sales.

Other press releases were sent out. Lists of key magazines, from *Mechanics Illustrated* to *Science News*, were compiled with names of editors. Brief personal notes to editors were sent with short stories about the Colorful Cobra Lily, the Sneaky Sticky Sparkling Sundew, the Passionate Purple Pitcher Plant and others.

"We found that many magazines enjoyed the news items and ran them. As they did, we coded our mailing address. That way we could tell which magazine pulled the most orders. Based on that, we checked the advertising costs and began advertising. Our ads were always simple, accurate, and to the point. We would show the plant itself and tell about its insect-eating habit, give a price, always postpaid, and wait for orders.

"The second year we had a mailing list so we prepared a four-page catalog using the same pictures we used in the ads. Every customer and previous customer received the catalog. We coded orders based on the dollar volume they ordered or whether they just wanted a catalog out of curiosity and never ordered anything. Future catalogs were mailed once to the curious. If they didn't order any plants, we dropped their name from the mailing list. If they did, we put them in the active file to get a new catalog each year and revised bulletins from time to time.

"Over the years, orders from florists and garden centers arrived. Naturally, a mailing list was put together to provide these potential customers with wholesale quantity prices. Slowly, but certainly, a repeat business was built."

Letters from foreign plant enthusiasts arrived. Many had seen the newspaper stories carried by the wire services. Some, like an angry British gentleman, only wanted to find a large-enough carnivorous plant to catch trespassing neighborhood cats. Others bought plants in quantity to sell to friends and neighbors. Some offered swaps of their oddities. Within five years, a worldwide clientele had been established.

Even more important, a select list of reliable growers that could propagate and provide other types of carnivorous plants became available. These new plants were offered to earlier customers who had begun collections of the oddest plants in the world, the meat-eating types. Business was, Armstrong says, really catching on.

From that point, new, larger, better-illustrated catalogs and wider advertising increased the company's sales. New markets were tested in schools, aimed directly at science teachers and college research specialists. Even with the extensive advertising, publicity remained the key to new customers. Letters from students and scientists alike led to news releases about their experiences with these botanical oddities. The more unique the experience and the article, the more publicity was achieved. And, Armstrong points out, the more publicity you generate about your business and your products, the more sales you can make.

Magazine writers, newspaper editors, and freelance authors wrote to the firm, asking for additional facts, figures, anecdotes. Encyclopedia editors wanted details for new editions. School publications wanted stories for their readers.

"It pays to provide the accurate, detailed information editors want. They're usually wonderful people. The better the photos and information you provide, the better and more extensive the story about your products. That all leads to more interest about these plants or whatever you have to sell. Sometimes, of course, you can feel mighty foolish the way an editor or reporter writes their story about you. But you must learn to accept these few disappointments along with the extensive benefits that free publicity provides. After all, giant corporations have dozens of public relations people pumping out their product publicity and their propaganda too. If they can do it and make it pay off, so can a small company. In fact, it's easier for a small company or an individual to put together interesting news releases. You know your products day-to-day and can tell about them more effectively."

During the first year, when sales were low, a tight rein on the budget was imperative. Armstrong collected old cardboard boxes from supermarkets to make his own shipping containers. He used plastic sandwich bags for packaging and still does, since the polyethylene plastic film protects plants, keeps them moist, and ensures their arrival alive to the customers.

"The man from Glad really had a message for me," he quips, while tucking another plant into a Glad sandwich bag with moist sphagnum moss for growing it in.

"The first few years were a struggle," he recalls. Lots of people, not the least his own family, thought he was in a somewhat nutty business, to put it mildly. Trying to get a bank loan for expansion, buying supplies, advertising, was nearly impossible. The local bankers just gave him a strange look as they ushered him out their office door. Cash flow was tight. Ads had to be paid in advance, and postage too, when the mailing was made. But those tight times provided valuable experience.

"When you're hungry you work harder, and when you're scared you run faster," Armstrong observes. "At least I did."

Many bankers may have chuckled as they shuffled him out their doors, but some didn't. One, a plant hobbyist at Manufacturers Hanover Trust Company, looked over the business and its potential. He recommended an accountant friend who also enjoyed unusual plants. Together they structured a business plan that provided cash in the slow season when catalogs had to be printed and mailed and ads placed, and allowed for repayment when orders flowed in during the peak sales season.

"Schools, both students and teachers, have proved to be the strongest base market for the plant oddities," Armstrong points out. From this base he expanded sales to science supply companies that sell to schools and school systems.

Over the years, new growing facilities were needed. It made sense to grow plants in the south where heating costs were low. Some growing could be in outdoor beds without greenhouses. A key to that phase of the business was his background on the farm. Farmers can spot other good farmers. And farmers like to grow a crop and sell it rather than get involved in packaging and marketing. Working with farmers, Armstrong organized contract-growing operations that could produce quantities of plants he needed when he needed them. The surplus was put in cold storage.

As the business grew in volume, it became obvious that an assembly line would be needed beyond what the family could do themselves. Rather than hire employees on a regular basis, Armstrong accepted the advice of his accountant to subcontract. His packaging operation has been and is today based on an old-fashioned but successful cottage craft approach, called subcontracting in modern terminology.

He contracts with teachers, factory workers, local mechanics who want to earn extra money. They buy their own supplies of bags, boxes, and packaging materials. Then they produce X amount of X product, whether in bags or pots or terrariums, and deliver them to the Armstrong farm. There the family does the final assembly and shipment.

There are no secrets of success to his or many other businesses he had seen or worked with, Armstrong believes. Most of whatever success he has achieved he readily attributes to watching and listening to the advice of successful businesspeople around him, and to his banker, accountant and wife.

"You should guarantee your product and stand behind it. When you sell an unusual item like a carnivorous plant, people may be intrigued but want to be assured that it will grow for them. We always have guaranteed live arrival and germination. In bad weather, just watch the weather forecasts as farmers always do. If a storm is coming, don't ship that week. You do get caught by freak storms and blizzards that freeze your crops and hurt profits since you must replace them, but you build loyal customers.

"UPS is good for shipping now that they cover the entire United States. They're fast and less expensive than regular parcel post, plus you have receipts for every package you send out. But they don't have heated trucks so winters are a mite hazardous for perishables.

"Customers often want to go into business in competition with you, strange as that may seem. It's part of the 'grass looks greener' syndrome. However, we see it as a good sign. There is a big market out across America. The more attention that is called to a certain type of product or plant, the more people learn about it. You eventually get your share of the total market if you stay on your toes and keep selling effectively.

"Some of the retail mail order customers are in effect in competition today in mail order. Their ads run with ours in mass circulation and specialty magazines. Although we may lose some direct mail order business, we still supply many of them with plants wholesale, and we're still friends."

Thinking back nearly twenty years to that Carolina swamp and looking today at the carnivorous plant customers he has cultivated around the world, Armstrong almost relishes his role as a plant nut.

"When you switch from something you know to an entirely new field, you're bound to make mistakes. Some hurt badly, others just sting for a while. But these years have been good, and fun too. We haven't starved, but we're sure not getting rich and probably never will be, at least not financially. However, when you can work right out of your own barn, take a day off here and there to fish or paddle a canoe or sit on the beach, that's riches too. When you can be home to watch the children grow up, see them play ball, work with them as they learn to function in this world, that's a bonus of wealth money doesn't buy."

Still crawling through the swamps around America, now taking photographs for audiovisual aids for schools to accompany the carnivorous plant kits, Armstrong hasn't really changed. He may have rerooted himself, but he's still a farm boy at heart and, no doubt, a plant nut to many.

12/Ed Mayo— From Accountant to Dump Lecturer and Artist

Ed Mayo was headed for a bean-counting career. He was graduated from Westbrook, Maine, High School in 1934, just a few years after the great crash of American business. Finding a job was difficult, but his ball-playing ability as a third baseman on the local semipro team proved the added plus needed to secure a job. He earned forty-two cents per hour, a total of $16.80 per week, for his first year as a clerk for the S. D. Warren Company in Westbrook. Working at the giant paper company's offices, Ed applied himself diligently to what he assumed might be a rewarding career in business, aiming to work his way through the office ranks. His third base prowess also paid off at $12 per week during the baseball season.

"I counted myself fairly rich during baseball season," Mayo recalls.

Trained in clerical and accounting work, he tended his

ledgers and otherwise counted numbers; backward, forward, and sometimes even sideways. It seemed to add up to a profitable, long-range career. After all, Ed reasoned, every business needed someone to keep their finances straight.

In addition to his training and work as an accountant, Ed spent time in the paper mill for extra income. He was settling in for a long pull in the bean-counting business world. During his years in office work, Ed attended night school to learn the techniques of drawing and art, which had long been a favorite hobby and pastime.

That creative outlet satisfied him at the time, he recalls. On the job, he progressed to cost accounting, inventory control, and other more demanding responsibilities.

Then World War II came along. It gave him several years at sea to ruminate about what he wanted to do. Counting beans, balancing columns of figures, and vegetating at a desk weren't among the choices topping his list of important things to do.

In the maritime service, Ed spent his three years from 1943 to 1946 moving things. "I was on transport duty," he explains. "We moved everything from beans to beer. And over beans and beer I thought a lot about what I really wanted to do."

There was no blinding flash, no great creative bolt of insight that triggered his decision to leave the business world of ledgers, records, and endless columns of figures.

"I simply decided that there was something else more important to do and that was painting and art," he says. Before the war, he had taken night courses at a school of fine arts. The move from being an accountant to being an artist wasn't immediate. When he returned from maritime duty, he had already decided that art was where he should concentrate his attention.

During the few years at sea, Ed had practiced lettering: plain and fancy, from simple signs to script-lettered scrolls. There was a need for that work in Portland when he returned. First came painting signs, lettering trucks, silk screening designs, and advertising messages for local businesses.

From 1946 to 1953, Ed developed a loyal following among businessmen and advertising agencies. He added to his staff as business grew. At the same time, he developed his painting abilities.

"It was a late start, at thirty years old, but designing displays, car cards, and other advertising messages was the easiest way to get into the art business and on my own," Ed recalls. He stuck with this transition phase of the art business for seven years. There was no great leap into the world of painting. Instead, it was a slow, tedious, and sometimes tortuous process. There was, of course, the sign-painting business, which needed his daily attention and which paid the bills. It also took years of his spare time, he admits, to reach the expertise he wanted as a sea and landscape painter, primarily in watercolors. He traveled the state of Maine, perfecting his abilities.

"Painting is art," Ed says. "The other work was the preliminaries, the staging ground to get from an accountant's desk to an artist's easel."

His high point, as president of the dump association, was yet to come. In 1953, Ed decided to move to what he describes as "one of the prettiest towns in Maine," Kennebunkport. He packed up his family, gave up his sign business, and moved from Portland to Kennebunkport, thirty miles down the coast. His home and studio overlook the Kennebunk River and its picturesque harbor with its fishing and lobstering fleet.

Today, teaching, painting and lecturing, Ed has the life-style he always wanted to become accustomed to. But even doing what you like doesn't always put even meat on the table. The classic lightning flash came to his fertile mind in 1964, at the town dump.

"That is where you really go to find the seagulls for your marine landscapes," Ed points out. "Some are around the coast, but if you really want to see them close up for artistic purposes, the dump's the place."

At the dump, the stroke of genius surged through him. He stood, staggered by his realization, palette and brush in hand; there was a subject that no one had utilized to its fullest potential.

"Friends and I would go down to the dump on weekends. It was folksy and fun. Dumps are common to many small towns. We would dump our trash, chat, and compare the tidings of our lives," Ed explains. "I'm an organizer at heart. You have to be as a painter, to put things together on canvas. So, why not organize the dump? I decided to form a Dump Association to promote interest in the fine art of dumping."

It is often difficult, talking with Ed Mayo, to determine if his tongue is ever out of his cheek. Nevertheless, the fact remains that, from that inspired day, Ed has created an international cult of dumpology.

People like and need to belong to groups. Lots of people, millions in fact, are joiners by their nature. They join book clubs and record clubs and local civic, service, men's and women's clubs. They are involved in environmental preservation groups, historic societies, church and garden groups.

It seemed logical that people might, just for the fun of it, join a Dump Association. So Ed Mayo started one. It's like the local yacht club or country club. If you can't or don't want to join a fancy club, you have an alternative, the Dump Association.

"To join our group, you must only be skilled in doing nothing," Mayo smiles. "After all, many clubs are mostly people that do nothing really."

The membership of Mayo's brainchild, the Kennebunkport Dump Association, is limited. It is not restrictive, he adds, just limited. There are forty members and lots of associated friends of the dump. Ed Mayo has been and remains the president. There are thirty-nine executive coordinator consultants who function much like typical club vice-presidents.

There are no dues or assessments ever. There are no required activities. However, the dump, by virtue of its professionally organized and promoted profile, has become famous, not just locally, but nationally and internationally. It has been written about in *The New York Times*. It has been covered by CBC, CBS, NBC TV networks. Newspaper and magazine stories have extolled its virtues. It has a symbol, a crushed garbage can marked KDA for Kennebunkport Dump Association, with a flower peeking out of the top of the crushed can and its lid askew. There are bumper stickers, membership certificates, Dump Credit Cards, and all the trappings and visual accoutrements of an ongoing, viable organization. Which, as Mayo is quick to note, it really is.

By using humor to lobby and lecture against littering, the KDA has made its mark. By carefully contriving to emulate more formal, prestigious organizations, the KDA pokes jolly good fun at our human status-consciousness and pecking-order foibles.

Since its inception, Mayo's famed KDA was ordained for notoriety. An annual report, based on the board of directors meeting, is carefully phrased in exact business English. It reads like a typical giant corporation annual report.

"Like most corporate reports, it doesn't mean a goddamn thing," Mayo explains. "Nor does National Dump Week, which is an annual function of the association. As leaders of the Dump Association, we realized, as politicians do and corporation executives do, it is much more important to make promises than to keep them."

However, the fact remains that National Dump Week has been proclaimed every year since 1968. It begins July 4th and lasts until Labor Day. This, Mayo believes, makes it the longest week of any nationally observed week of anything.

Having created the labyrinth of the Kennebunkport

Dump Association, it remained for Mayo and his dump-oriented associates to decide what objectives and goals should be achieved.

"We decide each year mainly to do nothing."

For Ed himself, the Dump Association has led to lectures nationwide about the work of the dump, the association, dumping, and dumpology. He enraptures his audiences.

In the meantime, a Miss Dumpy contest takes place each year, a highlight of the spring dump-picking season. All contestants must wear handmade costumes picked from genuine trash at the dump. There is, in conjunction with this event, a Dump Art Show, which is attended by hundreds. "Art critics have acclaimed some of the works better by far than that seen in the museums of New York, Philadelphia, and Chicago," Mayo says.

The annual Dump Parade, a recycled array of floats from genuine dump-picked trash, draws crowds from the Midwest, Canada, and as far away as California, Florida, and France. That too has its associated activities. As the parade of dozens of floats meanders through the winding streets from the school, through the town to its eventual destination, the dump, cheers resound for the dump's illustrious mascot, Ricky Rat. Bumper stickers sell well at the parade, proclaiming the dump as the "home of the friendly flies."

Mayo is active most of the year with his beloved dump activities. When he isn't lecturing, he is creating artifacts or corresponding with federal, state, and private foundation officials.

"Several years ago we filed an application for a federal grant. We asked authorities in Washington, D.C., for $500,000 for test borings and to complete the construction of our architect's rendering of a completely enclosed, glass-domed dump. Around it we plan to build the edifices for students of dumpology who would attend Dump U. They still seem to be shuffling the application around in

Washington last time we heard. Maybe this administration will finally recognize the value of dumpology.

"Mayor Beame of New York could not attend the bicentennial celebration of the dump," Mayo explains ruefully. "Instead, we received a red, white, and blue broom to help with the cleanup activities here. They also offered us several tons of authentic New York City garbage, but there was a strike then in New York, as usual, and they couldn't send a truck here with the garbage for our celebrations."

"The bicentennial celebration at KDA was a huge success, despite the missing New York rubbish," Mayo relates. "More than 6,000 people attended, and that was verified by local police department estimates of the crowds. There was, however, one rotten part of the event. No word had yet been received about the federal grant.

"If the federal government can give money to study dairy farms and conclude that cow manure is slippery; or can provide large sums to study cross-breeding of fruit flies and conclude that some have different-colored eyes after crossbreeding, why not funding for our dump?" he asks.

"For example, we did preliminary test borings ourselves to justify the grant we deserve. We discovered, at the 1776 level, the first traces of Colonial civilization in this area. Before that, people did live here, but they were too poor to throw anything away. At 1776, we found the first layer of artifacts. We knew it was 1776 because that first layer was quill pens. That was the year the patriots realized that swords were mightier than pens and threw away their pens to take up their swords in the cause of freedom."

Speaking at civic and service clubs or corporation conventions, Mayo becomes eloquent about his dump mission. He urges funding for a dump museum before modern technology buries all the beautiful relics of our history and heritage. Compacting trash is an evil, he believes. It destroys the honest evidence of our noble culture today. The museum, he continues, will be part of the Dump University. It will be pentagonal in shape, for reasons which are obvious to the militarily minded, he observes.

Rubbing one of the numbered, pretarnished bicentennial dump medallions, Mayo becomes reflective. He is planning another bicentennial celebration at the dump in 1978. He explains that the Dump Association established the bicentennial observance in 1976 by research, so why not establish 1978 as a new bicentennial date by additional research? “Research is wonderful, it can prove anything.”

Many products have been devised, created, or researched into being by the Dump Association. Blazers of members sport the filigreed, embroidered dump emblems. The Doctor of Dumpology degrees, coveted by many, are awarded annually following the tailgate party at the dump.

T-shirts, aprons, tote bags, and other paraphernalia all proclaim the existence of and tribute to the dump. Several musically inclined members of the organization are collaborating on a long-playing record, “Music to Dump By.” Trash trading stamps which are guaranteed to be absolutely worthless have been issued. For every full book of trash stamps turned in, the collector receives a free barrel of rubbish.

Another highly valued symbol of prestige in American society is reflected in the KDA collection of status symbols. A dump credit card permits all carriers to free dump-watching privileges throughout the United States and, through reciprocal agreements, at better dumps around the country. Thousands have already been issued.

These credit cards entitle holders to visit any dump in the country instead of using the roadside for rubbish disposal.

One member was asked for two credit cards before he could rent a car in Minneapolis. He had only one of the usual cards. That wasn’t sufficient, the clerk informed him. So he offered his KDA Dump Credit Card. The clerk, neither blinking nor twitching nor even checking the membership number, promptly filled out the forms and rented the member a car.

After years of study and careful observation, another dump landmark was reached. An official Dump Watchers Handbook was published in 1977. It has been issued initially in a limited edition of 1,000 signed and numbered copies. These handbooks, which provide much more than anyone really wants or needs to know about dumping, are available for $5.00 postpaid, from the author, Ed Mayo, of course.

His speaking engagements today range from civic and service to women's clubs. He has presented the story of the famed dump to such prestigious organizations as the Maine Medical Center Employee's Association, the National Court Reporter's Association in Washington, D.C., the National Association of Funeral Directors in Detroit, the American Public Relations Society, the American Paper Institute, and others. Despite his lighthearted delivery with tongue tucked securely in his left cheek, people do believe the reality of the unreal, Mayo explains. After each speech, some people always come to thank him, shake his hand, and ask for more intimate details about the dump, its history and heritage. He always obliges.

The dump credit cards are carried proudly, he estimates, in wallets and purses of government officials, congressmen, bankers, lawyers, mechanics, housewives, businesswomen and ecologists from San Antonio to Seattle, Hong Kong to Zurich.

"We must resist the urge to commercialize our beloved dump," Mayo emphasizes. "We could, for example, sell magazine articles to the Environmental Quality Commission in Washington. We've had requests from antique dealers for special dump-picking privileges, but they wanted to be notified and have specific items reserved in advance. We just can't do that. Equality is fraternity," he says.

Despite his prolific pronouncements and obvious sense of the absurd, many people do take the Dump Association seriously. Dignitaries have arrived to inspect the dump, only to be astounded that it and its associated members are far less impressive than they had expected to find.

One dignified New York official had driven the 350 miles to Maine to see what secrets might be revealed.

"It's nothing but a goddamn dump," he said disgustedly.

"We do keep the dump slightly cluttered to maintain a homey appearance," Mayo points out. "There are so few authentic open dumps remaining to compact life into smaller space and bury everything sanitarily, including man's mistakes, that we must preserve and protect that which remains."

One aspect of American society that stands out above all others, Mayo believes, is American gullibility. Believing that, he has set out to prove his point. His success speaks loudly for itself.

The publicity developed to promote the dump and gain it international acclaim has been skillfully tailored to top professional standards. Releases are in exact public relations format. A contact name is given. The letterhead is neatly designed. Headlines are graphic. Sentences, paragraphs, and punctuation are precisely proper and grammatically correct.

"When *Better Homes and Gardens* publicizes their award-winning home, a beautiful rose garden, a famed chef's recipe, it is always done in the best, most professional form. When giant corporations extol the virtues of their products or the talents of their executives, that too reflects the best the writing profession can put on paper to tout the firm. We have adopted the same professional style in all announcements about the dump."

The widespread coverage achieved in national newspapers, magazines, wire services, on radio and TV, is not attributed to the gullibility of the press, Mayo emphasizes.

"Instead, editors see the humor in the absurd and also understand the hidden antilittering messages buried in our dump news releases."

Every year, visitors arrive to meet the president and tour the dump. Mayo remains amused that after a decade of good-natured merriment, many people still become indignant at the sight of just a plain old dump. Perhaps they expected much more. However, most visitors occasionally appreciate it. When a sanitation engineer sees it after driving from Washington, D.C., or the Midwest, comments can be most unkind. They range from "what a waste of time" to "it's a fraud, we should file charges against whoever is responsible." Other comments would make a longshoreman blush.

The annual formal KDA banquet is attended in the best attire, from formal gowns for ladies to emblem-marked blazers for men. The evening is the occasion for awarding Doctor of Dumpology degrees, which, Mayo notes, has something to do with Ph.D. and even deeper meanings.

"Our message is simple," Mayo admits. "We try to educate through humor. Cleanliness is essential to survival. We're clogging our cities and suburbs with garbage. We have a use-it-up, throw-it-out and bury-our-mistakes syndrome in this country. That has been the American way, but we're getting deeper in the dumps every day we keep it up."

Mayo, poised with paint brush in hand, dump medallion as a belt buckle, trash tote bag over his shoulder and ready for action, also hopes to have the world's largest shareholder organization soon. He already has printed stock certificates, guaranteed to be worthless and non-negotiable. Each certificate is for 2½ million shares. When all are issued, there will be 625,000,000 shares outstanding, he points out.

Speaking has become a key factor in his annual income. The most-asked-for topic is the dump. His fees range from $150 to $550 plus expenses. Out of New England he expects $500 minimum plus expenses. His other popular topics cover butchering the English language and how to paint. As an accomplished watercolor artist and teacher, Mayo spends much of the winter months guiding students, both young and old, through the techniques of sea and landscape art.

A camera also has become an income-producing tool of his artful work. His "Kennebunkport, Maine, a Photographic Essay" has been hailed as a fine example of photographic art. It sells for $6.25 per copy, from Ed himself as well as from bookstores.

All his activities are an extension of what he sees as his native talents. They do indeed have their commercial aspects, but he's fond of eating and prefers to keep bank loan officers happy too.

"I do what I do and like it, both for the joy it gives me and others, and because it is lucrative. You can't separate those points," he says. "Fine art is painting. It becomes commercial art when you sell your painting. Both are necessary parts of life.

"We all sell something one way or another. It may be the hours of our time, what we make, what we do or say, assuming there's a need for what you do or say.

"There's so much to live for, so much fun to be had, so many things to accomplish, you might as well get on with what you really want to do.

"Everyone has worries and everyday frustrations. There are days the toaster hates you, and worse yet, you know it does. Most people are concerned with these everyday frustrations. Will the car start, did the cat get sick on the rug, is the rain going to spoil the picnic? Few really care that Russia and America can destroy each other twenty times over.

"Americans have a characteristic that helps them surmount their frustrations. It helps me when things don't go right. Americans can laugh at themselves. You may hit your thumb with a hammer and curse like hell at the time. Six months later, you'll tell the story about the hammer to a friend and laugh at yourself.

"Most of us live in the future and know it's got to be better tomorrow. That's also the American way," he muses.

The hard question: Any regrets? He shakes his head no.

"Were I to have returned to accounting and business, I could probably take early retirement. But I probably would not be in half the shape I am today if I had stayed at a desk job.

"We've raised a family, two boys and a girl. Doris and I have lived reasonably well, up and down at times, but that keeps you mentally awake. We had to keep our wits honed. We haven't accumulated lots of tangible things, but we've had a good life and we look forward to each new day. And we laugh at ourselves a lot too."

There is a zest to his living, an eagerness in his voice, his eyes, his posture when you talk with Ed Mayo. He loves his painting, his teaching, his family, friends, and beloved dump.

To his list of accomplishments—painter, photographer, lecturer, writer, dump president—perhaps one more should be added. Philosopher.

13/John Hackman—From Newspaper Reporter to Leisure Land Salesman

The smell of printer's ink was in the air with the first breath he took. His father before him had started as a journeyman printer and worked his way across the composing room to an editor's desk. All the years he was growing up, he knew he wanted to follow his father's career. Every day at dinner, he heard the hot news before anyone else read it in the next morning's paper.

There was something exhilarating in the beat of his father's typewriter. On vacation he frequently tagged along, watching the old man at work. He was often the first to arrive with his father at a fire, an accident, at the court as the judge pounded his gavel to announce a newsmaking verdict. The more he grew, the more his nose for news grew into an insatiable cub reporter's curiosity.

His first day in high school, John knew his first stop. It was the faculty advisor's office to meet the senior who was editor of the high school newspaper. John wanted a beat of his own on the school paper. Above all, he wanted a byline that he knew would eventually be seen by thousands alongside his father's well-known name. It would be, he felt, in bigger, bolder type, eventually.

As he watched other reporters race to scoop up news and saw his father beat them into print, or occasionally miss a scoop, he knew he could make a name as a top reporter. The feel for it was in his blood right to his fingertips. He knew it, felt it, smelled it. His nose for news told him so, even a fourteen-year-old nose at that.

Editing his high school paper as a senior, he stumbled onto what he thought was the first big scoop.

"A bunch of cheerleaders and football players were having a party. Today you could call it a swinging singles party. I heard about it and borrowed a pair of binoculars. A reporter from our school paper went with me. He checked license plates while I watched the frolics in the woods. If I had brought a camera along, I could have had some super shots for *Playboy*, except there wasn't a *Playboy* magazine then. In fact, all I had was a story that no paper would dare print, just a wild party that led to a few pregnancies."

That nonscoop didn't hold him back. He kept his nose for news pointed toward a journalism career. With four years of college, good grades, a journalism degree and the recommendations of college day employers, he signed aboard a local paper as a cub reporter. The pay seemed only pennies per week with rent, food, car and other expenses, but the name of the game was grab the byline. He meant to grab his share.

From that first paper, after a few notable bylined stories, he landed in the newsroom of a larger city daily. From there, with proven experience added to his résumé and clips pasted in his presentation book, he took on more important assignments. From the police beat to night court, from real estate developments and zoning battles to a society column he wrote, Hackman's bylines became well known in his area.

Reporters live on a treadmill. Chasing the big byline stories keeps many of them running faster all the time. "It's competition every hour," Hackman explains. "You must beat the other papers, scoop your competition, get the inside quotes, exclusive ones if possible. And," he adds, "make damn sure your stories are good enough to get a byline whenever possible.

"The action on a paper isn't in the city room; it's all around town. If you're good at digging out the facts, the figures, and rolling over stones to find what news may be buried there, you can build your reputation. Depending on how well you write the stories, you may topple politicians, or conversely, help put others into office. The power of the press is enormous. There is no doubt that politicians can be built up or shot down by the public's reaction to what they read in their newspapers."

Hackman didn't believe in distortion. There also are laws of libel that kept him from straying too far from the actual facts, although on occasion he may have added "local color" to a story or two. But adding that extra vivid dimension of description, was one of his strengths. He had studied reporting styles of the best, big city, "name" reporters. He understood how they could turn a phrase to capture reader attention. He perfected and honed his own sharp style.

Occasionally, Hackman's wife would needle him. She didn't believe all she saw in print. She knew him and his job, with its pressured deadlines, well enough to realize that his stories tended toward the sensational. Despite the cries raised occasionally about "inaccurate quotations," Hackman admits he pursued his increasingly slick style, even when fellow reporters sometimes questioned his tendency toward the overly dramatic.

His wife also became more picky as she read his accounts of events that she had attended with him. "She began to ask me if that really was the same meeting we had attended," he recalls. "She'd needle me with comments like, 'That was only part of what he said. You left out some of the most important comments.' "

Undaunted, he continued to probe deeper and more doggedly during interviews, assuring himself that his passion for the truth and the public's right to know justified his approach.

Although he winced when reporters labeled him a maverick at times, he pursued his own style with increasing enthusiasm. After all, he reasoned, he was getting the bylines. And, he had assured himself, the larger the headline, the more frequent the byline, the faster his promotions would come.

"What stopped me before I became really rotten was an assignment that put me into competition with three of the best reporters from out-of-town papers. They were covering a candidate for governor," he recalls. "I was on the candidate's side, politically. He was a friend and could help my career if he sat in the governor's chair. I tended to overlook some facts about him. To be honest, he wasn't a bad choice for governor, but he wasn't Mr. Clean either. But then, who is?

"The other reporters dug into him, asked pointed questions, and their stories played up what the opposition said. Actually, they were giving readers a more balanced approach and coverage than I was, but that didn't dawn on me at that time," Hackman admits.

After several months on the campaign trail, Hackman sat down at his favorite bar to commiserate with himself and his city editor. By then, the campaign had turned around and his favored candidate was losing in the public opinion polls. "I was feeling sorry for myself, more than for my candidate," he recalls.

As Hackman tells it, "I was sitting in the bar, rehashing the campaign and getting really steamed about the great image the other papers had created, I thought, for the opposition. About the third drink it hit me.

"Sure, I was mad at them, whoever 'them' is. Actually, I was mad at me because I had lost. I began to realize what they reported was the hard facts, and on balance, they were just doing their job. I was the one who had begun to distort things with my own special style and my own personal viewpoint. That would be fine in the editorial page or in a commentary column, but not in the news I was supposed to keep unbiased.

"When I went back and read some of my stories, I could see how silly they must have sounded to anyone who compared my stories with others. Maybe I had dreams of glory and thought of myself as a syndicated columnist already or molder of public opinion or whatever," Hackman admitted. "I decided to take a few days off, to clear my head and get over my mad, both at the lost election and at myself. And," he confesses, "to think about what I really wanted to accomplish, and the best way to get there without looking like a fool in print."

Hackman read about a vacation community being built in the Pocono Mountains of Pennsylvania. His wife had written for literature, so they decided to spend a day in the area and unwind for a few more in the mountains.

With his wife and children, he headed for the Poconos. The gates to the four-season development were landscaped beautifully. The salesman that greeted them was friendly, not too pushy, intent but low key, Hackman recalls. The model homes were handsome and attractively appointed. He readily admits that his defenses were down. They enjoyed their free meal and the tour of the facilities that had been built. His wife and he examined the architect's plans for the ski lodge, tennis courts, swimming pool, lakes that would be built when the stream in the valley was dammed. Beaches would be added for swimming, docks for boats, a dance pavilion for parties too.

"We looked it over carefully. I had a reporter's eye to see what most people don't see. I had that nose for news that pointed me in the right direction to dig out stories where nobody else smelled them," he says.

He listened intently to the salesman; analyzing the smooth talk against the facts he saw. As they examined building sites, walked across home lots on the mountainside or along the proposed lake, he did some mental arithmetic. He studied the sales log, counted the number of lots that had been sold. He divided by the number of salesmen and multiplied that figure by their percentage commission per sale.

"They were making ten times what I was making. They didn't work nights. They lived nearby. They had the best of all worlds," Hackman says he believed at the time. It seemed so. A reporter seldom ever hit the high road, an annual salary of $50,000.

He reasoned he could write and talk as well as any salesman there, could phrase a sales pitch just as well, and paint word-pictures of the beautiful life in that four-season recreational community with its pure, pine-scented air, fun in the sun and skiing winter wonderland. He could write their brochures better than they could, he thought to himself.

Hackman applied for a salesman's job his last day in the Poconos. His credentials covering real estate were short, but he wrote his résumé again, slanting it to his advantage. If the sales manager wanted another smooth-talking sales personality, he was that man. With his background, he was able to pass the real estate salesman's exam the first time around, after a brushup course on Pennsylvania real estate law.

"I became a new pioneer in less than ninety days," he points out.

He left his reporter's job with no regrets. The daily deadline pressure was off his back. Hackman fully realized that he wouldn't have his cherished bylines, but figured he could always freelance for papers and magazines to keep his fingers exercised. The commissions he would pocket for leisure land sales, he admits, may have blinded him at that point.

For several months, he had his daily "ups" in the development office. Each salesman had their turn at "up": stand up and take your turn at the next prospect that walked through the door. If your up was on the board when a deadbeat walked in to eat and drink and then say no, that was your down for the day. The ads that ran in New York, New Jersey and Philadelphia papers promised every joy of country living. All the prospective buyer had to do was clip a coupon and drive out. He was given $5 gas money back, a barbecue meal for the family, and a leisurely but well-structured tour of the community-to-be. Everyone that arrived was a winner. They took home a set of picnic dishes or a cooler chest, a clock radio, an electric blanket. Winners were happy. Happy winners were easier to sell. Those incentives lured the masses in, Hackman notes. "They came by the hundreds every weekend."

If you were lucky, your up might yield a susceptible prospect. The symptoms were easy to spot. Ohs and ahs from wives as you glowingly described the larger-than-Olympic-size swimming pool to be built, the property owner's free ski lift passes, songs around the roaring fires at the community center when winter winds wailed. You could spot the buyers, he points out. "They tuned in to your frequency and began to talk among their family about the swimming parties, the sailboat races, the barbecues and snowmobile trail rides. They would begin to echo some of your own phrases.

"If they wavered, we had some great closers to get them signed on the line. Statistics proved that if they didn't sign that first visit, few returned to buy. We had to get them primed and signed. When you had a hot one on the line you didn't want him to wriggle off the hook," Hackman explains.

One of the best closers of a sale was the car-radio gambit with the sales manager. Hackman would gauge how a prospect reacted to a given lot, any given lot. If he seemed susceptible Hackman would call the sales office and ask about that lot. The sales manager would hold him off a moment. Then he'd crackle back on the radio to say another couple was in the office trying to decide on lot 204 or 591 or whatever number Hackman had called in. The sales manager in turn, with appropriate concern for Hackman's prospects, would suggest that they should put their names in right now if they didn't want to lose that beautiful wooded lot. He might insert "tree shaded," "lakeside," "brookside," "mountain view," "secluded," or whatever other key word or phrase best described the number on the master map.

If that appeal didn't work, Hackman had a bagful of others. His reporter's experience told him which to use and when to try which on for size.

"The escape appeal worked effectively too," he points out. "If a family came from a large city, escape from the city streets to fresh air, sunshine, pine-scented woods usually led to a signed contract.

"If they liked sports, you emphasized the skiing, snowmobiling, tennis, fishing, hunting, horseback riding. You could zero in on their interests and rifle-shot your sales pitch right to the heart. If they drove an expensive car and were professional people, you talked land investment, appreciation of land, capital gains. One phrase always helped close deals with doctors, dentists, and executives," he recalls. "I'd remind them that 'they weren't making any more land these days.' Most had read about land values rising. They could visualize renting their chalet to cover mortgage payments, seeing it appreciate in value and become money in the bank for them.

"Older people were more concerned with a quiet, peaceful living, low taxes, and conveniences. For them, we emphasized the nearby shopping mall, free snowplowing in winter, the friendship of other older couples at bridge or shuffleboard or in the arts and crafts center to be built. We always avoided mentioning the hundreds of screaming kids they would have for neighbors."

His income climbed dramatically the first few months. If land was such a good investment, he convinced himself, what better place to invest his surplus money than in land where he would live. He could turn them over later at a profit and pay taxes on only half the profit as capital gains. Hackman sold himself. He bought more lots. Living never looked better. He hired an architect to design their new four-season vacation home. His wife began shopping for new furniture. His children hiked and picnicked, played tennis and went fishing.

Their new pioneer career lasted all summer. He sold lots of lots. Money grew on the trees in the Poconos, he believed. Projecting his monthly commission earnings, he saw a $40,000-income year. That would be more than three times his reporter's salary.

"Someone pulled the plug in the early fall," Hackman explains. "Most of us salesmen didn't notice anything strange. Maybe there were fewer trucks on the roads and not as many workers cutting brush for new streets," he recalls, retracing the events as he has done a dozen times, "but we kept on selling lots. Some lot boyers even ordered prefab homes. The materials arrived and were staked on cleared parts of their lots. Many families came up on weekends from the cities to picnic and look around. They often brought friends who also bought lots. One couple that had bought their building lot from me helped me sell lots to six other couples that they knew.

"Two salesmen quit in late October. They just left. Both had been selling land for years at one development or another. I figured they moved on to greener pastures or maybe had made enough that year to take time off.

"My nose for news wasn't sniffing right," he says with a slightly pained expression as he traces the next episode in his disaster. "I should have smelled something, especially when one of my customers complained about not being able to get a building permit. I shrugged it off as a typical small-town zoning-board screwup. I was too busy thinking up new words to add to my sales pitch to worry about a building permit."

Another customer complained the next week. His problem was a building permit too. A few letters arrived, asking when the local township, in which the new community would be built, would issue permits. Hackman asked the management. Nobody knew, but all assured him it was typical small-town politics, a delaying game, nothing more.

One fateful October Monday, Hackman and his family were in the new community center building, already roofed over and closed in well ahead of the building schedule, looking at the architect's renderings of their proposed new home. They decided to break ground immediately. With luck, they could get the foundation poured, the walls erected and the roof on before winter arrived. On weekends they could work on the inside themselves. By spring they would be at home in the mountains, new pioneers who crossed the Delaware for a new life of prosperity in their own new frontier.

Next morning, Hackman went to the township building inspector personally. He had dealt with hundreds like him, small-town bureaucrats. Now that he was putting his roots down permanently, he might as well meet the locals and get this matter of building permits settled. That meeting was more of an encounter than he anticipated.

"First thing I learned," he remembers ruefully, "the township had not even approved final plans for the proposed community itself. In fact, they hadn't wanted it, had not approved it, and intended not to let it become reality if they could help it. Not only weren't building permits being issued, but some township officials and their friends intended to drag their feet through every court in sight. They wanted no part of several thousand new people. It was that simple. The lines had been drawn and none of us knew anything about it.

"The next so-called official I talked with had a more

impassive attitude. He just folded his arms across his chest, shrugged helplessly and guessed we would all have to see what happened."

Hackman called his architect, the mason he had picked to pour his home's foundation, the carpenter and plumber. No one would admit knowing anything about the delay. Looking back, he never was quite sure what they knew or how much they wanted to admit. They had their own roots in the area and relatives on local boards as well. He should have realized that, but he was city and they were country.

After three weeks of digging into files, public records, correspondence, and legal documents, when he could spare the time from sales, Hackman learned about those good old "just country folks." He compares that search to walking on a lake full of Jell-O. No matter where he stepped or prodded, there wasn't any firm ground. Everything seemed to quiver, including himself.

"I asked so many questions of the land development company executives that they treated me as an enemy in their midst, but I kept asking," he points out.

In reconstructing the events from start to final messy finish, Hackman swears he never really believed the developers had planned a skim and run deal.

"We received our commissions when we signed a customer and they paid their deposit," he explains. "Some people paid full cash to avoid time payments to a bank. We received full commissions on that. If a family or individual put down a deposit and planned to pay the balance in easy monthly installments, the bank paid the developer, and we got our commissions then. Either way, we saw a steady stream of money. It all seemed reasonable. The lot prices were high, but roads had to be built, and all the amenities too."

"About the time I smelled the proverbial rat, other lot owners were finding their way through what turned out to be a colony of rat tunnels."

Hackman called old reporter friends. They helped him dig. Eventually their stories broke, with banner headlines. The developer had left town. His company was insolvent or nearly so long before all the lot owners were even on the court calendar.

Roads could not be completed or sewer lines laid, or water mains installed. There was no money for those projects, or any others; the pool, tennis courts, the lake, etc.

If roads, sewers, and necessities could not be built, no building permits could be issued. That meant no houses could be built. Lots that sold for $5,000 to $15,000 each, depending on the view or proximity to the promised lake, were inaccessible and unbuildable. Screams of outrage resounded through the Pocono Mountains when the stories ran.

"If only," he remembers thinking a thousand different ways. If only he had double-checked the facts. If only he hadn't gotten greedy. If only he had put his commission in the bank. If only he hadn't sold their former home and used the money to buy more lots. If onlys still haunt him today.

There were more than enough tearful sessions with his wife, his attorney, his banker, and the lawyers representing his customers, who tried to heap a share of the blame for the disaster on his head. Legal fees alone reduced his bank balance substantially. His only luck was that he too had been caught when the development went sour. That, his reporter's background, and promises to help dig out the facts and hunt down the guilty made him an ally, rowing in the lifeboat with his customers.

The final story on that pleasant Pocono valley has not been written yet. Four years have passed. Attorneys representing hundreds of lot owners are still comparing notes and revising briefs for future court cases. Investigations have been launched by county, state, and federal authorities. It still is not clear who did what to whom, or when or how. Millions of dollars changed hands, one way or another, in cash or signed documents that banks still hold over the heads of lot owners.

Hackman is no longer a new pioneer. He's back on a reporter's beat, living in a rented home in his old hometown. He decided to stick with writing after all and let the new pioneers scale the mountains in the Poconos or cross the plains to search for golden futures by themselves.

"You can keep your new pioneering. I tried it once and that was once too many. Those Indians out there in the mountains not only scalped me, they damn near cut my head off."

Perhaps John Hackman's new pioneering spirit died in the Pocono Mountains. Perhaps he never really had a real pioneering spirit. Factually, back in the original pioneering days of the Wild West, many who tried didn't make it either.

14/Philip Peters—From Commuting Executive to Camp Operator

He rode the antiquated Erie-Lackawanna for fourteen years, rattling from his pleasant oasis outside the city to his high-rise office building and back again each night. Although the Erie was often late, the Summit branch of the merged Erie-Lackawanna railroad was usually on time. He liked that. He prided himself on being punctual and methodical in his daily habits and in business. It had paid off handsomely. He made $21,800 annually, less taxes.

The express left at 7:10 A.M., arrived mostly on time in the bowels of the Hoboken railroad station. Philip Peters boarded the Port Authority Trans Hudson tubes for the rapid ride under the river, transferred to New York's spray-can-blotched subway, and was normally in his office, sipping coffee and reading the morning's mail, by 9:15. By 4:54 P.M. he was headed home, away from the turmoil of the job and city, shoulder to sweaty shoulder with the maddening mobs in the subway and PATH tubes. The tubes actually arrived in Hoboken a full half hour before his train left for home. That allowed sufficient time for one extra-dry martini in summer, a perfect manhattan in winter at the railroad bar in Hoboken Terminal. He had developed the common commuter's ability to elbow his way through the four-deep crowd, order his drink, sip and savor it leisurely before walking down the platform to catch the 5:45 train home. If asked what he saw on subway or tube on any given day, he could seldom remember. Going to or returning from work he was blissfully oblivious to the crowds around him.

Dinner was usually at 7:20. His wife was also methodically prompt. She was loyal, an excellent shopper and chef, and a loving mother. Aside from occasions when she snapped back about her bad day, which sounded worse than his bad day, she was an understanding, good listener. She was also, when the spirit moved her, a most resilient bedmate. They were in tune with each other and the life they had carefully chosen. It suited them and they suited it.

They had two cars. One was a dark green station wagon that matched the dark green shutters on their colonial home. It served its purpose well, chauffeuring the children from school to Little League or Girl Scouts. It held the twice-a-month groceries and functioned as their vacation vehicle for trips to explore their state and those around it. The five-year-older car had been repainted dark green, to match the shutters also. There was no point to leaving a new car at the station in rain, sleet, and snow.

Phil Peters had been methodical and on time as a matter of course through school, college, and in the army. His two-year army tour of duty wasn't challenging or threatening. The measured march of military life suited his temperament, he had been studiously punctual all his life anyway. His father had been a banker, accustomed to opening the doors at nine and closing them at three, rain or shine.

Meals had always been on time too in his youth. His

wife, whom he had married when they were both twenty-one years old, had been a childhood sweetheart. Her father was head teller in the bank in which his father had been the mortgage officer up to the time of his retirement. Their families owned cottages at the same lake in the hills of New Jersey. They spent their summers there, growing up, falling in love, getting married at the rustic rural church they attended those summers of their youth.

Each morning, Peters awoke to John Gambling, the son, on WOR radio. He had listened to John Gambling Senior before trudging off to school years before. He would put two slices of toast, one white, one whole wheat in the toaster, while the water in the pot boiled his three-minute egg. Juice and coffee completed his breakfast before he drove the car from their driveway to catch the morning train.

"There was really nothing wrong with my routine," he emphasizes. "Some people may believe that we had a dull life. That's far from the truth. We had a routine and stayed with it. We explored more rivers by canoe, hiked more parts of the Appalachian Trail, saw more national parks than anyone else I know. We just happened to be in tune with each other. We knew what we wanted and went after it in our own way."

In winter, when the sun comes up later, Peters was on the train before his children were out of bed. He was in Hoboken before they left for school. When they were young, he arrived home after they were in bed. That didn't disturb him for many of those years he rattled back and forth on the Erie-Lackawanna.

"It bothered me when I couldn't be home to watch Jess in a Little League baseball game, or see Jeanie at a play, but I was a commuter. I had my job to do and it was in New York. To give them the opportunities of living in a nice town, I accepted the fact that I would be away each day for twelve hours. We had the weekends and vacations plus holidays together," he points out.

Actually, Peters didn't mind commuting. He rather enjoyed it. He was able to read the *Times* and the *Wall Street Journal*. During the week he scanned trade publications, plotted his day's activities, and on Fridays organized his weekend.

"I enjoyed my job. From a management trainee, I had been given opportunities for advancement that the college recruiter had promised when I interviewed for the company on campus in my senior year. I had been assigned to various departments, purchasing, sales, even shipping. I had always thought shipping was something for a clerk. It wasn't. We had to coordinate trainloads, estimate loadings, arrange siding time at warehouses, worry about deliveries of components so the assembly lines kept humming smoothly at the factories. One carload of chemical solvent arriving late could throw a factory's schedule out of whack for several days. That cost money," he emphasizes. "I learned to appreciate what it takes to keep a big corporation running right. I also spent time in accounts payable and accounts receivable early in my training program, and later with trainees under me."

Peters wasn't one to set the world aflame. He didn't make waves. He didn't stand out in a crowd. He did his job as methodically and conscientiously as he could. He was reliable and dependable. He was paid twice a month and in turn paid his bills on time.

Two dates stand out vividly in Phil Peter's memory. One alone might not have made him a new pioneer. Together, they changed his life and life-style.

"There was a really great old guy on our commuter car," Peters recalls. "We called him the 'Mayor' of Summit. It wasn't a joke at him, it was more a salute to him. He was, thinking about it, much more methodical than I was. We caught the same train each day. We sat in the same car, three cars behind the front car. He always sat on the left side of the front aisle seat. I preferred the middle of the car because you didn't feel the bounce of the wheels as much.

"I had been commuting for eight years at the time. It

was late November, the first miserable, slushy snow day. Winter was early and messy that year," Peters remembers. "Anyway, the guys in the car decided to throw a party for the Mayor. He was retiring that week. Get this," Peters emphasizes. "He had been commuting for thirty-six years . . . on the same train, from the same town, in the same car. I asked some of the guys, Charlie Polanski and Bud Brill, if he had really ridden the same railroad car all those years. They assured me he had."

Peters marveled at the old man's resilience. He knew he would be on the train for the party, so he joined the planning committee. They arranged streamers. One commuter who worked in the art department of the telephone company offered to have banners made. Another regular took up a collection. One of the historic-minded fellow commuters and a railroad buff began compiling milestone dates about the Erie-Lackawanna that would, they hoped, relate to the Mayor's recollections of his commuting years.

"The party was a grand success. Someone even sprang for a case of champagne. We were well on the way by the time the train pulled into Summit that night," Peters says. "It was a helluva great party and the old guy really enjoyed it."

By rights, that fellowship of commuters should have reinforced Peters' methodical approach to life. Commuting was like a club. You met people on the train that you saw every day. You got to know them. Some you didn't see socially, but then when you spend almost four hours every day on the old rattler, you get to know people pretty well. Many commuters, probably most among the millions who ride trains, buses, or in car pools would probably agree. The commuting world is a world you share with many several hours every day, but that is all.

The second event that changed Phil Peters' perception of his life, his career, his real desires for the years ahead, didn't hit suddenly. It sneaked up on him.

He had been talking with a banker the week before

about the cost of living and rising interest rates. He had talked the day before with a stockbroker about tax shelter bonds. One morning he sat with a neighbor discussing money, taxes, and inflation.

"We were comparing notes on our wives, the usual stuff, how much they spent on clothes, on food, on trips to the beauty parlor. We complained to each other about the way the money came in one big check and then went out faster than we could figure where it went.

"One day we listed our commuting costs alone on a notepad. That's probably when I first began to add up the facts about my life," he observes.

To simplify his figuring, Peters rounded out his commuting to ten full years. Over the next few days with Bob Brill, a neighbor, he put down figures, the time and money they spent just commuting. The more the dollars added up, and the time, the less sense commuting made to him.

"You can add it up yourself," Peters urges. "I left home at 7:00 A.M. and arrived in my office at 9:15. That's two hours and fifteen minutes going in. I left the office at 4:54 and arrived home by 7:20. That's two hours and twenty-four minutes. Total it up. It's four hours and thirty-five minutes every day. Now multiply that by five days a week. It's twenty-four hours and thirty-five minutes each week," he points out.

Peters multiplied his twenty-four hours, thirty-five minutes of weekly commuting time by the fifty weeks he commuted. Rounding the figures out, he calculated that he was on the way or returning home more than 1,225 hours a year. For ten years, his commuting time was 12,250 hours.

"Now for fun," Peter explains, "divide that by ten hours, figuring that's what you have each day minus time for eating and sleeping, if you didn't commute. In ten years, I figure I had lost 1,225 days out of my life."

Peters thought about that. He also calculated the cost in dollars and cents of commuting. He rounded out figures because train tickets had varied, always upward in price, as had the tubes and subway token prices.

Average monthly commuter ticket $50. Multiplied by twelve, $600 annually. Fifty cents each way in the tubes each day is $5 per week times fifty weeks . . . $250. The subway cost $2.50 per week, averaged out over ten years. That's $125 more.

The raw cost of commuting totaled $975 per year. Peters explains that that's just the raw cost. He added on the cost of eating lunches out in the city. "You can't be an executive and take bag lunches to work. It's bad for the image of a rising executive type," he jokes.

So he added the meals up too, a conservative $5.00 per day, $25 per week, $1,250 per year. Add tips to that at 15 percent—another $187.50. Add on New York City sales tax on meals, $62.50 per year. Putting those figures together he arrived at $1,500. The more he added up the time and money spent commuting, the more it bothered him.

"Then," Peters says, "add up the New York City sales tax for anything you buy, clothes and gifts, and the New York State income taxes you pay for the privilege of commuting to a wretched place to earn your living." Only one state seemed higher. It had earned its reputation as Taxachusetts. New York State was not too far behind. Even giant corporations were fleeing to the suburbs or other states. Peters began to think about flight too.

"When you're spending $975 a year just to commute, and $1,500 to eat plus 1,225 hours a year to do it, somehow I began to believe it didn't add up right," he admits.

"When I thought it out and extended the projections of one year through the thirty-six years the Mayor had commuted, I began to feel sick. There had to be a better way," he reasoned to himself.

Today, Peters runs a camp. It began as a cross between a family motel and a camp for youngsters. It isn't making him rich, but he hasn't had to add up the score of commuting for a long time.

"In summer, we would use part of our vacation to take the children to summer camp. We looked forward to it and they did too. We would drop them off, then tour one of the New England states by ourselves for a week, before heading home. At the end of the eight weeks of camp, we took our second week of vacation and traveled with the children before school began," Peters recalls.

The camp was nothing fancy. It contained twenty more or less reasonably maintained cabins nestled in the Maine woods, with its own private sandy beach on a pond. The mess hall, caretaker's cottage, recreation hall, and other buildings were rustic. Rustic is a favorite realtor's word for slightly run-down.

"The camp owner always claimed the moss growing on the shingled roof helped keep the cabin waterproof," he laughingly recalls. "Actually, at his age, he was just making another excuse for not keeping up with repairs, painting, and basic maintenance. At the end of camp, six years ago, we were the last to leave. Bert, the owner, and I were talking while the kids collected their last few treasures. He asked jokingly why I wanted to go back to the city. I really didn't have any answer, because at that point, I really didn't want to go back to the city," Peters remembers.

They sat drinking another cold beer when the owner asked point blank, "Why not stay here and buy me out?" Peters thought it over on the drive home. For weeks he worked out financial projections, discussed the idea with his wife, toyed with visions of becoming a Maine guide. During Thanksgiving school vacation, the Peters drove back to the north woods camp. Asking price was $55,000. Peters estimated another $10,000 minimum would be needed to do the repairs he knew were necessary. He added another $5,000 for good measure, based on building material increases.

True to his methodical approach, Peters wrote to other camps, collected literature about camp operations, gathered data from camp owner associations. In the state of Maine alone, he discovered that summer camps have been an almost invisible industry for the past seventy-five years. A 1976 survey revealed that Maine now has 234 children's summer camps serving more than 73,000 campers each summer. Camps have a $46.7 million annual economic impact on the state. Of that figure, $19.1 million covers direct operating expenses. The 115-page phase-one report, "Children's Summer Camps, Their Economic Value to Maine," provides many other current figures. The tourist industry in total is a billion-dollar one.

When Peters first began seriously considering a new life-style for himself and his family, assembling hard facts was difficult. His research included gathering facts from real estate people with camps for sale. "You need a sense of humor and ability to translate their descriptions," he points out.

He wrote to state tourist boards and chambers of commerce where they existed, answered ads for camps to compare their prices, costs, literature, and facilities. He analyzed different types of camps: those for children, private residents, and day camps.

Children's camps provided organized, planned activities and learning experiences for youngsters. Some were well known and prosperous. Others, he discovered, seemed on the verge of termination. Family campgrounds, too, offered potential for a livelihood.

Peters spent his entire winter writing and calling realtors with camps for sale. He asked for profit and loss statements. He questioned the condition of buildings. He asked about camper enrollment figures for ten years back to see whether a camp's trend was growing or falling off. He corresponded with owners who had their family motels for sale.

By the following spring, Peters and his wife, June, had made their decision. They had checked maps, traveled to see sites, talked to realtors and owners. They discussed the philosophy of the camp and proposed transition periods with the owners.

"We asked more questions than some of the owners

wanted to answer," June Peters recalls. "We checked into state standards for water, for health, the need for a full-time registered nurse or practical nurse. We asked about former personnel and who would be available again as regular staff."

Eventually the Peters picked their camp. After all their methodical surveys, they bought the one they knew best from their own children's experience. The key to its purchase was the owner's willingness to stay on for two more years as director and adviser.

"We wanted to have a guide to walk us through every step, from buying food to recruiting new campers for the coming season," Peters points out.

The money from sale of their suburban home bought the camp. With that equity, the Peters family borrowed against the camp for improvements, secured by the buildings, land, furniture and fixtures.

"The first summer we got to know the staff and children. Our kids were great. They knew the inside story of what needed repairing, which boats leaked, which cabins had rotten boards in the floors," Phil Peters recalls. "My wife loves to sew. I'm glad she has that skill. It saved us at least a thousand dollars sewing old drapes and making new room dividers. My ability, limited as it was to driving nails, cutting boards, replacing shingles, saved us carpentry bills.

"Thank God for plastic pipes. They made plumbing easier. When the old galvanized pipes burst between the well and our mess hall, all we needed was a backhoe to cut a trench. We simply curled the plastic pipe around roots and boulders and covered it. We used Sears' finest pipe," he quips. "All I needed was a sharp knife, a screwdriver, pliers, and a hammer to be a plumber. Plumbing inspection in the 'out back' isn't what you face in the cities. There aren't unions here either," he adds.

The Peters prepared a checklist of priorities for refurbishing the cabins. Four larger ones separated from the others were top on the list. They were remodeled as family camp units for rent by the week, month, or season to individual families. Peters believed this would provide solid income, including off-season fishing and hunting facilities.

"Insulating those four cabins proved worthwhile," Peters points out. "We now can rent them for ten extra weeks each year. A small wood stove in each provides ample heat. I also rent boats and canoes and snowmobiles in season. That additional income from the extra weeks gave us working capital to upgrade the other buildings."

The first two years, camper enrollment held steady. His wife did the cooking. He did the cleanup. First year figures showed a net profit of $8,425 before taxes. Their second year net climbed to $12,340. The Peters spend winters writing thank-you letters to parents of former campers. They prepared a periodic north-woods newsletter. Its purpose was to encourage repeat attendance and attract new friends of previous campers.

Results surpassed what they expected. Their homespun stories of a wandering mother bear and cubs, an encounter with a roving moose, visits by a porcupine family that invaded their cabins, captured the imaginations of former campers, particularly their parents. Descriptions by June and their children of massed flights of migrating ducks, the ice fishing expeditions, snowshoeing hikes in winter, brought a response they hadn't anticipated.

"Families began asking whether they could come up to visit in fall, to see the colors; in winter to ice-fish or hunt, in spring for white water canoeing."

Today the Peters no longer have a children's camp. Their other cottages all have been converted for private family vacationing—camp style. The cabins are roughhewn, with double bunk beds in smallish bedrooms. Peters had to hire the backhoe to dig water lines deeper so they would not freeze in winter. He bought more wood stoves and cut ten cords of wood per year.

When roads are bad, he trucks families to the camp in his four-wheel-drive Dodge. On occasions he's even picked them up by snowmobile for their week's snowbound vacation.

What began as a grand plan for a children's camp has turned completely around into a family camp cabin community, if fourteen cabins can be called a community. Peters credits his success to what he once shunned, a Christmas letter.

"June and I never liked the idea of Christmas letters. Either they were all about a family's glowing success or the opposite, tales of all the tragedies that befell that family during the year. When we started our north-woods newsletter, we tried to make it informal and friendly and just tell about the world around us. The kids added thoughts too.

"Maybe we sounded enthusiastic or just lonely off here in the north woods," he laughs. "Whatever it was, each time we sent one out, we received more letters in return. Actually, those newsletters were run on an old mimeograph machine. They turned out to be the best advertising we could have done."

Methodically figuring his expenses and adding up gross income, Peters keeps his records as neatly as he did in his offices, long forgotten, in New York. He even keeps a diary of the winter weather, funny things that happened, who caught the biggest trout, and when the maples first begin to change color in the fall. These notes were added to their monthly newsletter.

From his ledgers, he figures his income was only $15,430 last year. The truck, of course, is written off against the family company. So are the canoes, rowboats, one motorboat for towing water skiers, four snowmobiles, CB radios, and other equipment needed for their business.

"My taxes are lower and my accountant makes certain that we pay our fair share and no more," Peters emphasizes. "Even with the write-offs, we're too small for the IRS to audit. I hope," he adds.

Sipping his coffee, watching his youngsters as they disappear into the woods on cross-country skis, Peters says he doesn't really miss commuting. However, he did drive his family all the way to Portland, Maine, two years ago. They stood on a bridge and watched the Freedom Train roll into town.

"That's the closest I've been to a train in six years," he muses. "And the closest I really ever want to get." Then he turns back to his typewriter to begin another newsletter about the cross-country ski races he and his family plan to enter, starting with the suggestion that some of their friends come up during the February school vacation week that is scheduled.

"If you figure fourteen cabins full in one week, multiplied by $75 per week, off season rates, that should be enough for tuition next year for our oldest son," Peters says.

Life in the north woods as a new pioneer adds up to contentment for the ex-commuter. At Christmas time, however, he still enjoys watching his son's electric train run round and round the tree. Occasionally, he admits, he puts a passenger on the flat car and watches that model man go round and round and round.

15/Fred Pomeroy—
From Utility Company Lineman To Zookeeper

Someone, he can't really remember who, had once told him that the best career would be with a company that provided a service people needed every day. That conversation was so far back in his youth, he doesn't even remember it distinctly. It could have meant the water company, the fuel company, the electric company, the telephone company. It meant, he was sure, a company that provided something people had to have regularly.

As he grew up and went through high school, his grades weren't especially notable. He worked well with his hands, received high marks in shop and other classes where things seemed practical. Foreign languages and math held no interest. He never expected to travel to foreign countries, and if he didn't, he reasoned, a foreign language was a waste of time. Math didn't seem to be useful either.

His school was near open fields. He preferred to watch

geese fly north in spring with flocks of ducks close behind. He walked to school, whatever the weather, because he liked to walk. The open world of field, stream, lake, and forest was what he enjoyed. He watched the seasons turn, went fishing and hunting in season. In winter there was ice fishing, trapping and other more interesting pursuits than the formal studies his parents emphasized.

As graduation neared, he remembers, he didn't have any idea what he would do next. College was a luxury and no guarantee that he would find a good job, people had told him. What he should do was get a steady job to make some money. That sounded logical. After all, he was rather fond of money. There hadn't been much of it around the house in the years of his youth.

From far in the back of his mind, as he tried to decide what he wanted to do, the discussion about getting a job that gave people what they needed every day surfaced. There was room for trainees as power company lineman. He applied.

The qualifications were reasonably simple. You didn't need much experience, even in electrical work. The lowest level on the utility lineman's ladder was at ground level. Before you ever got to climb a pole, you cleared brush. For that, he was loaded with experience. He had cleared brush, lots of it, around their home and on neighbors' farms. He had chopped down trees, cut them up, split logs, and stacked endless cords.

With the hunting season coming up, he figured that a lineman's job, clearing brush, running across animal trails, and locating new hunting spots might lead him to the best deer or bear of his life. And, he realized, cleared land opened up new ground for smaller game: rabbits, partridge, grouse. If you enjoyed the smaller game, you could get better shots at quail in the open as they fed on berries by the flockful.

There were few applicants for the job and fewer who could take the labor it involved. The first few months he understood why.

"We didn't use chain saws then," Pomeroy recalls. "It was ax and bucksaw and your own sweat that cut the trees and cleared the brush. There were no handy highway wood chippers to gobble up the smaller brushes. You cut them and burned them . . . from the time you hiked into the power lines until you practically crawled back out at night."

Despite the hours, blisters, pulled muscles, and other hardships of the job, Pomeroy says he actually enjoyed it. The outdoors was his chosen kingdom. Working here, he found the deer trails, the bear dens, the places he could hunt rabbits, squirrels, and other game in abundance. Even in those pre–World War II days, hunters tended to stick close to main roads and work the edges of them. He knew the way in and out of the happier hunting grounds because he left his blaze marks in any area where sign of game promised better hunting.

Eventually, he rose up the lineman ranks, climbing poles to check for electrical outages. He uncoiled miles of wire to help keep the lights alive in homes fed by the utility service. The higher he climbed, the higher his pay rose. That is the difference between unskilled labor—clearing brush—and the skilled work higher up the ladder of success, he reckoned.

As a boy, he had enjoyed animals. He collected them, a baby raccoon and a nest of ducks that had lost their mother to a snapping turtle.

Despite his mother's attempts at persuasion and periodic corrective measures, he collected snakes. They fascinated him. So did turtles, toads, and assorted lizards. He recalls one winter day spent in the house alone, trying to scrub away the stink of a skunk that had not proved as tame and loving as he had expected.

A lineman's life wasn't all that wearisome. It kept him where he wanted to be, outdoors. As the years added up, however, his income didn't. You can climb only so high on that type of job. There were opportunities for indoor work at better pay, but desks were things he had left behind when he left school.

"I finally met a girl that liked the things I did," he explains. "No matter what they tell you, two can't live as cheaply as one. She liked the outdoors and animals. She liked everything I liked, except the winter and the money my job paid. So, we packed up what we had, which wasn't really all that much, and headed south."

By the time they reached the Carolinas, the climate was more to his bride's liking. The land and landscape were strikingly similar to what they had left. Instead of northern pines and firs, southern varieties grew, interspersed with southern types of oaks. Instead of puckerbrush of the north woods there was scrub growth of the typical southern piedmont. Otherwise, the hardwoods and softwoods were a similar mixture. They expected to blend into the fields and forests, settle down and find employment.

"I was born a Yankee and sounded like one," Pomeroy recalls. "My accent was so bad and theirs so southern, it was difficult to understand each other. They sure didn't seem to know what we were saying. Back then, over twenty years ago, a Yankee wasn't the most acceptable form of life even in the Carolinas."

Linesman or related jobs may have been available. Southern accents seemed to carry the day when they were.

Luckily, their knowledge and love of the woods made them some friends, despite their different accents. Hunting time brought friends to their door and invitations to go gunning after doves instead of quail, raccoons instead of squirrels. Along the shores of lakes, they set blinds for ducks and geese. He remembers feeling like a pioneer even then, bringing game home to eat when cash for shopping at the stores was short.

His zoo just grew, Pomeroy believes. At first he and his wife had no intention of becoming zookeepers. True, they could mend a wing, help heal an animal's broken leg, or care for a motherless fawn. As he treked the woods, fields, and swamps along the coast and explored the mountains inland, he made more friends. He'd swap an orphaned bear cub he caught for a young calf. Bit by bit, snake by cow by sow, Pomeroy assembled his menagerie.

Years back, cash and credit weren't what they are today. Bartering for what you needed or wanted with others who needed something that you had was a normal procedure. It certainly was with the original pioneers.

When they first settled in their new area of the Carolina coast, the Pomeroys farmed some while he pursued a variety of employment opportunities. There were shoes and clothes to buy, a family to feed, and other necessities of life that required cash.

The idea of a roadside zoo wasn't a streak of bold genius. It was more a gradual outgrowth of their fondness for animals and the outdoors.

"People, lots of people, in fact most people, enjoy animals." Pomeroy points out. "They like to see them, learn about them. As more people move to cities they have less chance to see animals . . . our native ones and other types as well. Only a few larger cities have zoos. It seemed a natural thing to us to start our own local zoo." They did.

With rough-cut lumber, farm fence wire and other inexpensive building materials, Pomeroy and his wife began building lodgings for their first animal arrivals. Within a few years, they had their first displays completed. Visitors stopped in, paid a nominal fee, and let their children watch.

A traveling circus, on the verge of bankruptcy, needed a home for some of its animals. Pomeroy accepted them. Another circus offered a somewhat aging lion in exchange for two young bears born on his place. They swapped. As more customers arrived, the Pomeroys added a small gift shop.

A pigmy hippopotamus, some llamas, a zebra, more bears were added to their pet collection. Big animals, they began to realize, have correspondingly big appetites. In addition, new regulations had been drafted. New, improved quarters were required. That required more buildings and more land.

At times, the animals may have eaten better than they did themselves, a neighbor observed.

"We may not be getting rich, but I never really expected to," Pomeroy states flatly. "We like animals, we enjoy what we are doing, and we expect to continue building for our future here."

There have been some unexpected upsets along the way, like the time when their retired circus lion escaped. Feeding time was in the morning, when Pomeroy routinely picked up chicken parts from a nearby poultry processing plant. The parts had slight blemishes, a bruise or torn flesh, which made the birds unpackable. He picked them up along with other parts that his carnivorous pets would eat. When he returned to his lion's cage, the old beast was gone. A neighbor had heard strange rumblings in the woods nearby. Instead of his lion, Pomeroy found state policemen with loaded shotguns and 30-30 rifles. They didn't seem overly eager to go lion hunting that morning, through scrub oak and pinelands, recalls Pomeroy. "However, hungry beast or tame pussy cat, they had their orders."

Rather than lose a friend, Pomeroy selected two tender, well-plucked chickens, and headed through the woods.

"I felt foolish, making loud, purring sounds, but it was that or have my lion shot. I only took an hour to find him. He was sleeping beneath an old pine tree . . . just as peaceful as you see them in the *National Geographic* pictures of the African plains.

"The police were pleased, I guess, when I came walking back with the big cat trotting alongside. That episode was both good and bad. The bad was we had to sell our big cats. The good was the newspaper story, thanks to an editor with a sense of humor and a vivid imagination, that appeared in our local paper. Other papers reprinted it. Busloads of people arrived; from school classes to a ladies group touring the country. That made me realize you need stories about your business to attract people."

Pomeroy scratched his head many nights, thinking of ways to attract people. He didn't want another lion hunt. He didn't want any problems from neighbors. What he wanted was traffic—paying customers coming through the turnstile he had installed in his gift shop leading to his roadside zoo beyond.

An opportunity arrived in a truck early one morning. Another hard-pressed circus had a feeding problem. Their elephant was perpetually hungry and hay was too high priced. Pomeroy had loads of hay. He also had room in a large paddock for the beast, so he acquired the three-ton elephant.

Several weeks later, he too had realized that the elephant, although friendly enough and trained to do some crowd-pleasing tricks, was an accomplished hay-eater. Bale after bale disappeared.

He had just thrown the fourth bale into the feed bunk when some youngsters came to visit with their parents. They were eating sandwiches neatly wrapped in plastic sandwich bags. They had almost not stopped, their father explained, but the children had seen the elephant's trunk twitching over the top of the paddock fence.

Pomeroy visualized the headlines. He could move the elephant up in front of the fence where it would be a leading attraction. How many elephants are there along the Carolina coast? His lucky streak stretched one step further. The father was a farmer. As they watched the elephant devour half the bale and throw the rest around the ground and on its back as well, they talked.

"He had a few cows with the same bad habits as my elephant," Pomeroy relates. "They messed up more food than they ate. To solve the problem and get more efficient feed use as he planned to do anyway, that dairy farmer had switched to hay wafers as big as your palm and about a half inch or so thick. As he told me about it the kids kept eating their sandwiches. That's when the idea came to me."

Pomeroy contacted local farms until he found one that made hay wafers for their herd. He hired students to pack them in plastic sandwich bags to keep them fresh. Price per bag was twenty-five cents. He drew a line on the ground outside the elephant's enclosure and marked a bulls-eye inside the feeding trough. The idea was to have his customers throw the wafers in the trough, not at the elephant. It worked.

Not only did it work, but he reduced the cost of feed to zero. He even showed a profit. Customers bought the wafers that fed the elephant.

Pomeroy extended that thinking to his other animals. He began packing grain and other feed into bags and boxes, plastic cups and containers. The cost of feeding the livestock dropped drastically. His profits increased.

Once an idea dawns, it pays to follow through to explore all other avenues in which it can be applied. Pomeroy scratched his head a lot more in the next few weeks.

Manure is great for growing crops, he knew. It cost him time and money to clean up pens and dens. His elephant alone left meadow muffins so large that a week's deposits filled a pickup truck.

Pomeroy sent out the word to local editors. He offered exotic manure, at first for free. People came with pails and buckets, garbage cans and boxes. They hauled away manure all one day. More people came to see the zoo. Two organic gardeners offered to buy all the elephant manure he would sell. He priced it at $1.00 per garbagecanfull at first. The price is up to $3.00 now.

Costs had been a problem for many years—food costs, cleaning costs, housing. By the simple expedient of selling input and output of his animals he had cut his overhead, increased his profits, and saved time. His notoriety, thanks again to friendly editors who must have chuckled as they typed their stories, brought more business. It also brought new opportunities to swap species and exchange specimens with larger zoos. He took to training animals for other zoos.

Reptiles had been an early love. His snake pit was a drawing card. Back in his early farming days, Pomeroy had remembered his grandmother urging his grandfather to use every bit of each hog they butchered, even, she had joked, making a purse from the old sow's ear.

That thought came back to him one day when a visitor inquired, innocently enough, what he did with the snakes in his snake pit. Snakes may not have ears, but if you can use everything from a pig but its squeal, there must be something you can do with snakes besides look at them as a curiosity, he reasoned.

Pomeroy is in the snake poison business too. A snake milker who knows how to extract poison from the fangs of his rattlesnakes, copperheads, and cottonmouth moccasins buys the precious juices his snakes emit. With gentle, careful stroking the expert herpetologist collects the venom. It is used by laboratories in antitoxin work for snakebite victims.

From the first lean months with their simple roadside zoo idea, Pomeroy and his wife have built a thriving business. His gift shop has been expanded to five times its earlier size. Local crafts are displayed and sold. A pet store has been added where they can teach others love for animals of all descriptions. Sales are limited, at this point, to fish, turtles, toads, skunks, and tiny lizards.

Pomeroy may have become a new pioneer slowly, year by year, but he had an old pioneer's eye for opportunity. People bring the strangest ideas and odd things to him every week.

"A visitor came back after visiting islands in the Caribbean and the South Pacific. He had pictures of what he said was an authentic shrunken head. We put them on display. He saw that we had some crafts made out of seashells and asked whether we wanted different types of shells in quantity," Pomeroy says with a smile. "I really wanted more shrunken heads.

"However, after thinking about it, we decided that shells could sell well. We could make things with them. People liked to collect them."

Today, shells from the South Sea Islands may arrive periodically. He bleaches them in old bathtubs, then spends off-season winters with local craftspeople handcrafting them into necklaces and shell lamps. For Christmas, shell wreaths adorn his door and store. These sell well too.

Pomeroy hasn't ever had another lion hunt. His elephant attracts paying customers and earns him many friends. Youngsters by the busload come from schools with their teachers to learn about the world of animals he loves. Although he admits to dreams of a safari into Africa, he has what he considers the next best thing. He can explore the world of animals he loves right in his own backyard.

16/Tom Risch— From Handyman to Chimney Sweep

Mary Poppins was not exactly his favorite movie. And he really can't sing as well as Dick Van Dyke, or dance as well, for that matter. But he's dancing a happier tune to the jingle of money in his pocket since he gave up the humdrum world of home handyman for the fun of chimney sweep.

Like a lot of people, after graduating from school he had done the usual things while the hours, days, weeks and years droned along. He actually hated school, he admits. After high school, there was no compelling reason to go to college. The year after high school, he lay around, bored with himself and life, not doing much of anything. He painted houses and hated that too. He didn't like a nine-to-five schedule or even a boss, for that matter.

The fact is, he really didn't have any direction, so he experimented with painting, carpentry, general fix-it work.

Aside from his independence, he admits he was getting nowhere.

While working on an attic, repairing a chimney, he found an old top hat. Putting it on, he tried a lusty "Chim Chim Cheree," the song of the happy chimney sweep from *Mary Poppins*.

The lady owner, recalls Risch, came out to find out what the racket was all about. When he had finished, she asked him whatever happened to the old chimney sweeps. He hadn't thought about that before, but being a curious sort, he finished the chimney repair and drove over to his local library.

There he spent some days researching chimney sweeps. The local fire chief, when asked about it, said simply, "Hell, son, there ain't no chimney sweeps around," and then added for good measure, "What are you doing to keep busy?"

Tom Risch decided to become a chimney sweep *extraordinaire* that day, he says.

He really didn't have his roots planted in much of anything. A handyman career wasn't exactly a path to fame and fortune. But, he thought, after all, Dick Van Dyke did earn a lot of money, and he danced on rooftops with a top hat and a chimney-sweep broom. So, why not?

Luckily, an old-timer in upstate Connecticut had been a chimney sweep. As old-timers do, he spun wild and sooty stories about his days on rooftops. Listening to him, Tom Risch solidified his decision. He would become a chimney sweep, circa 1972.

He researched the topic more thoroughly. The potential seemed enormous. There really weren't any chimney sweeps around any more, he discovered. Equally important, people were installing wood-burning stoves and looking to other ways for alternate energy to beat the high price of conventional home heating.

From oil furnace dealer to library, from mason to telephone directory, Risch continued his search for information and know-how about his career-to-be.

Several months later, he had bought a used vacuum truck, repaired it, and obtained a variety of odd-looking brushes and tools. To tell the world that he was finally rerooted in a real business, he placed a classified ad in his local newspaper. It read, "Chimney sweep for hire." One of the first potential customers asked him how he proposed to keep the horrible black soot off her new white rug. Others asked questions for which he had no easy answers. In fact, he soon realized he had few answers at all.

Risch might have been discouraged. But he had hated painting houses, and school, and the humdrum of being a general fix-it man. What he did have was perseverance and a need to be independent.

A friend came to his rescue, not with money or ideas, but with work. He let Risch practice on cleaning a chimney.

"He left town for a few days," Risch recalls, "because he couldn't bear to see me teeter around on his roof or face what I might do to his chimney."

After a day's labor, covered with soot, grime, and layers of whatever else had been caked inside the chimney, Risch completed the job. It seemed to him at that time that the business of chimney sweeping was something he should avoid like the plague.

But Risch has a stubborn streak in him. Worse than he hates to paint houses or go to school, he hates to be beaten.

Jerry-rigged equipment, although it looked as though it might work, wasn't the answer, he discovered. It took him several months of phone calls around the country to line up equipment that would do the job. Meantime, he built himself his own vacuum cleaning system. He redesigned his advertising, read up on chimney sweeping, and gathered together whatever information he could find. For a young man who hated school, those six months may have been the most studious in his life.

Raring to go, he tried ads again. This time he had answers. The work went fairly well, and he was paid. He received more replies to his ads, and word-of-mouth compliments about his work helped too.

Four years later, with top hat and tails, smiling with the charm and grace of the nineteenth-century chimney sweep, Tom Risch had made his mark. He taught himself his business. He now teaches others.

With experience behind him and a catchy new name, August West, which he feels attracts the customer's attention better than his own, Risch has developed a chimney-sweeping system. He has put together a package of equipment, from large, industrial-size vacuum cleaner to brushes, rods, scrapers, poles, and a top hat to cap the package. He may not have enjoyed learning in school, but he's turned out to be an exceedingly successful salesman and teacher himself.

In the past few years, dozens of people have come to him, to study his methods, purchase his equipment, and begin their own careers as chimney sweeps under his tutelage.

"If it works for me, it can work for others. What I learned the hard way, and the dirty way, I can teach others," he says.

"I like the work, first. I love the down-to-earth people who put out efforts to chop and stack wood to keep their home fires burning. I like the image of the nineteenth-century sweep, and I enjoy the smiles when the job is completed.

"And not least, I like the money. I earn $40 for the first flue and $30 for the second in the same building. If I clean the usual four to five chimneys a day, it's a tidy bit of business," he notes. Other sweeps, his protégés, agree. A weekly income of $400 to $500 is not bad money.

Decked out in top hat and tails, Risch has set off to fill what he sees as a growing need for a professional chimney-sweep system across America.

"There are more than 25 million fireplaces in this country," he says. "Basically, they're dirty as hell. There's forty years of soot in many, because nobody has been cleaning them for years.

In his system and kits, there's a soot sweeper. It has a four-inch-diameter hose and power enough to suck all sorts of soot and dirt into the vacuum as it is brushed from the chimney. He offers a brush kit with chimney-sweeping brushes for all size and shape flues. There's a tool caddy to carry the tools of the trade, flexible rods to bend around corners in a fireplace chimney. These are rigid enough to force the brush up the flue or down.

He offers ropes and weights, ridge hooks, and even a top hat. The kit costs about $1,400, without the truck to haul it, of course.

There may be truth to his predictions that chimney sweeps will sweep up handsome incomes in the years ahead. That will depend, of course, on each person's ability, energy, and desire to go after the business.

This much is certain, he and others like him have seen blue sky in a few short years. And they're sweeping the dark clouds of soot and debris out of chimneys to have not just blue skies smiling at them, but green in the bank too.

"The market for chimney sweeping is huge and growing," Risch says. "What it takes is education.

"The advertising I've used here in Connecticut does two things. One, it tells people they have a serious problem in their home and unless they have their chimney cleaned they face the real danger of chimney fire. I use outside, authoritative sources for this message . . . people like the National Fire Protection Association. And two, my advertising makes them smile. I've heard of chimney sweeps working in coveralls and trying to present themselves as servicemen. Well, they're right, it's a service. But it's a much more attractive service when the guy doing it looks like a nineteenth-century tradesman, with all that that implies: honesty, simplicity, a high degree of dedication, and a sense of humor. All these qualities are sadly lacking in the business world, but I felt that as a chimney sweep I had a golden opportunity to bring some of them back. I think I can say it's paid off . . . in the form of happy customers and a healthy bank account."

Not content just to teach new sweeps the fine art of cleaning up—both soot and money—Risch also turned to writing. He felt there weren't enough sources of information about his new love, chimney sweeping. So he wrote a book. That may seem strange for a kid who hated school, but he has a way of talking straight to the point. He knows the questions people ask and puts the answers down clearly and to the point. His book sells for $9.50. From it, a person can learn the basics of chimney cleaning. Risch also finds the book a selling tool for the equipment he has assembled, designed, and now markets.

The August West Soot Sweeper has a patent pending because of its unique design. A brush kit, tool caddy, his trademarked Quik Connect Flexi Rods, which he plans to patent, rope and weights are available. His sales for the initial tool kit for $150 are growing well. His advertising kit with materials to begin an ad campaign, complete with artwork, is for sale.

Risch offers on-the-job training too; several days watching him at work, learning the basics and the fine points of turning up a chimney until it's whistle-clean. Those who sign up for this minicourse for $300 can learn how to use the equipment, customer-cultivating protocol, and how to service chimneys to keep customers happy. He caps the minicourse with a New England dinner.

Tom Risch is branching out too. When he isn't poking his brushes up a chimney or vacuuming debris away, he's devising new and better ways to sell his services. It's not a franchised system, he explains. It's just the necessities a person needs to set himself or herself up in a business of their own. He really sells a system of independence, he believes. It's based on his experience and the research he has pulled together from equipment manufacturers, his own designs, and the knowledge he has gained from others around the country.

There's a sparkle to his eyes even when they are rimmed with soot from a hard day's work. His customers are happy, his protégé ranks are growing, his kits are selling, and his bank account is adding up.

With top hat on and neatly pressed tails in place, Tom Risch heads off to pursue his new career each day. Like the sweeps of the nineteenth century and the pioneers who crossed the plains, he fits the picture of a new pioneer.

17/Dennis Hardy—From Attorney to Boat Mechanic and Marina Operator

The world is full of lawyers. They are everywhere, besides their law offices. They greet us practically at the cradle, and follow us to the grave. When you buy a car, a home, even a television set, some lawyer has drawn up the pretty printed words in those contracts and sales agreements. When you sign anything, to make it legal, binding, and a permanent part of the record, a lawyer is required almost every time to phrase things just so to the satisfaction of parties concerned. In any contracts between parties, there are usually two or more lawyers attending, smiling and bound to uphold the law as they see it. They're a happy bunch.

Defending yourself against an unjust traffic ticket or your dog running loose may even require an attorney in court. Corporate lawyers, divorce lawyers, tax lawyers; there are specialties in every field, and that includes the law. In county governments, state assemblies and senates, the federal government, lawyers reign supreme.

The law in all its majesty, with justice prevailing above all else, is a magnet to many. It is a good life for those who follow it. There are few poverty-stricken attorneys. They rarely sue each other, either.

Those thoughts didn't really cross the mind of Dennis Hardy while he was serving as a young naval officer. He had graduated from Colby college and entered the navy's officer candidate school. While on active duty he toured Europe and the Middle East. The navy was a chance, he recalls, to see places he had never been. It was exhilarating.

Raised by parents who worked hard for a living, he had been urged to get a good education. He did. So did his brother, who is working on his Ph.D. in education. "My father had worked with his hands at shipyards all his life," Hardy says. "He put in thirty-three years at one government shipyard or another. He worked hard and well. But he always wanted us to get an education so we could work with our heads instead of our hands. Dad realized the value of an education more than we did at the time, I suppose."

During his navy tour of duty, Hardy had time to think. "At sea you get a lot of time to think. I thought about my future, my options. College days were over, the navy offered experience I could probably get nowhere else. Law school also was an option that held some fascination."

He had always been active in the outdoors. Sailing was a special pleasure, which may have come from his youthful association with boats and his father's occupation. The navy offered challenge and a chance to really see the world. The ads, to Hardy, seemed to be fulfilled as he toured countries he had only read about.

Bright, witty, in good shape physically and mentally, Hardy took some long looks ahead as he sailed aboard a navy cruiser. Years back, military duty was perhaps a sterner life and much less well paid. Today, the modern military, intent on building its volunteer strength without a draft, is offering incentives that must have mystified old salts.

The law looked better, he recalls. In early 1968, Hardy left the navy in Norfolk, Virginia, and took time off to think about his long-range goals. He sailed a forty-four-foot boat with friends along the California coast down to warmer Mexican waters.

In the meantime, his father was retired and looking quietly around for an activity that he and perhaps his son might pursue together. The Hardy family was quite close-knit. They had their usual share of minor differences, but on balance, they were close. "My parents are from the old school," Dennis observes. "They believed in sacrificing to help their children get launched better in life."

Arriving home after his cruising, amusing time in West Coast waters, Hardy discussed the future with his father. He already had his college degree, so the idea of a law career seemed logical. To help pay expenses, he needed a work base. Luckily, the nearby seacoast town of Wells, near the Portsmouth, N.H., navy yard, was dredging its harbor. The town selectmen were trying to locate someone to develop a repair and marina facility that would help bring business to the harbor and the town. Large corporations (as prospective lessees) wanted more, perhaps, than the town (as potential lessor) was willing to relinquish. Young Hardy took a long, hard look and decided to take the gamble.

"It was a chance to get my feet wet in a business while I went to law school" he recalls. "The terms seemed reasonable since I was willing to work with the town officials within the framework of what they wanted to accomplish at their new pier and harbor area." A deal was made.

In 1968 Hardy invested his entire savings to build a small combination repair shop, showroom, and living quarters for himself—one room in the loft. He had actually made the decision when he committed himself to a three-week mechanics school in Milwaukee run by Evinrude Motors. He was in business as a franchised dealer for their engines, working his way to a law degree. "I had a liberal arts education, with no background in mechanics or business at all," he remembers. "In fact, I was totally untrained for what was ahead of me. That three-week school gave me sound basics. The rest I had to learn, day by day, the hard way."

His first building and investment in the initial stock of engines, manuals, and parts devoured his $6,000 savings. From that point on, he had made a commitment. It was make the business go or there would be no money to pay for law school.

At the same time, however, Hardy kept his options very much alive. He attended law school for three years at the University of Maine in Portland. He studied four days a week, then spent Fridays and weekends at his small marina. The building had a roof, walls, and windows on a slab, plus plumbing and a septic tank. During the week, he took a room in Portland, returning to tune, repair, and sell engines on the weekends.

"Luckily winter is a slow time for boat and engine work, so I could spend all seven days a week on papers, briefs, studies, and other efforts to learn the law." During that time, Hardy looked forward to a comfortable office, serving clients, helping them overcome the obstacles in their lives. Every hour spent over a sputtering engine made the practice of law look better to Hardy.

He passed the bar exams and became an attorney in the State of Maine in August 1971. Immediately, he and a law buddy began the search for suitable quarters. They were on their way. Time, money, energy, and sleepless nights had earned their degrees. But bits and pieces of his background prompted extra-serious thinking.

Hardy has worked at many things along the way to his attorney's parchment. He had traveled through Canada, working on wheat farms, picking cherries in British Columbia. He has worked in offices and factories too. There seemed to be something appealing in the business of working with his hands. "When I was young, I had always felt somewhat insecure. For example, I didn't join the Boy Scouts for a while because I was afraid of getting lost in the woods on a campout. I don't know what I was really afraid of, but the feeling was always hanging around, right over my shoulder," he explains.

He adds, "I spent a lot of my life running ahead, looking over my shoulder. I can't really explain why. Maybe I wanted security or maybe I was afraid of failing in something. So I kept running ahead. That probably accounts for my constant drive to accomplish something, to see something tangible get done."

His engine repair shop and the marina with its boat service facilities was small, as that type of business goes. But it did give him a sense of accomplishment. It also helped pay the bills for law school until the glorious day when he could give up the grimy work and put on the proper suit to appear before the bar of justice, serve his clients well, win esteem and acclaim.

But the practice of law and its allure of fame and fortune was not what he had expected. Hardy was losing interest in that career.

"I had some cases and took a good look at the legal system as it exists today. It's a mess. It's insulting to people who expect and require the most of it. Much of it is unfair," he believes.

"The delays are intolerable. Even Shakespeare wrote of this in Hamlet's soliloquy on the insolence of office and the law's delay. Things haven't really changed much in all the years. People must wait in line hour after hour to hear the guilty party beg off the charge again and again with postponements. Those with justified grievances must go back again and again and again to court, wait, and finally realize that their adversaries tip-toe lightly away with a tap on the hand, while the aggrieved end up out of pocket and frustrated.

"Judges may have compassion, but the technical loopholes of the law too often let the victims suffer and the guilty walk away untouched. Time is wasted and wasted and wasted. Even in seemingly simple civil cases, which comprise 60 to 70 percent of a local lawyers work, delays and complex human relationships hamper solutions. I've seen enough of it, enough to convince me to leave it alone," Hardy says. He walked away from it completely, all the way back to his marina.

Perhaps this realization, as he watched trials and civil cases come to dead ends, triggered his decision to give up law practice and the promising, lucrative career that could have been ahead. More likely, it was a combination of factors in his nature. One part of him wanted things real and fair and honest. Another part enjoyed accomplishing tangible goals and being away from the animosities and human problems associated with legal work.

"When you tinker with an engine, tune it up, you see the end results, it runs. When you repair a boat and the customer feels it smooth again in the water, those are the results I like to see," he explains. "You can do your best in court before a fair-minded judge, but lose a case because a technicality lets a wrongdoer go while the victim stands totally astonished by the whole procedure.

"There are always frustrations in whatever you do. I prefer the frustrations of solving a problem here with these tools, using my head and my hands, and seeing the job get done right. The legal system seems almost contrived to circumvent justice. What may be legal," he adds, "is not always right or fair."

Hardy didn't drop out. He values his education and his law experience greatly. It has given him an appreciation of the world around him and the people in it, and a sense of fair play and responsibility. It also has enabled him to pursue his chosen life with a greater understanding of the many people with whom he deals daily.

"Training for the law is training to think, see opportunities, sense when to wait, when to move ahead or back off.

In reality, I just decided that there were more important things I wanted to do, to accomplish" he says. "If in the marina business I'm lucky enough to get ahead, it's just so much the better. I'm outside most of the time, from March through December. Operating a marina is like having your own physical fitness program, especially when you do a large percentage of the manual work yourself."

Working steadily from the time the first fishing boats leave in the morning, until dusk, putting in many seven-day weeks, has not bothered him. He has thrived on it. "What I'm doing isn't really work," he explains. "When you like what you're doing, it isn't work. If you would rather be doing something else, then what you are doing *is* work."

For several years, he lived in the first building that he helped erect himself. Several years later, still during law school, he and his father erected a larger shop, a thirty-by-sixty-foot metal truss building with a steel roof with fourteen-foot eaves.

Local folks thought it was much too big. Besides, wood was the accepted building material in this historic shipbuilding area. Some even shook their head about "that young lawyer who fixes boats, what's he know about 'em." Dennis looked ahead. He knew the building was bigger than well-meaning advisors said, but he had found his ground. He was putting new roots down deeply. He recalls feeling an exhilaration, an expansionist confidence: "I'd had a chance to make comparisons, explore my options, look around for opportunities. I knew this was what I wanted. Once that was settled, and the seeds sown, I really dug in and knew this could all work out the way I wanted it to."

The area grew steadily for years. Even during the Vietnam conflict, the economy held surprisingly strong. "Despite the recession a few years back," Hardy says, "there has been a steady growth in recreation, buying habits, in demands, desires, wants by consumers. It just seemed to me that with an ability to provide the services people wanted, I could make things move my way." Three years after he built the shop he built a sixty-by-one hundred-foot boat storage building, all metal.

Looking back to his first few years, Hardy often retraces the steps he took after the decision to uproot a law career and settle by the sea with his engines, boats, and marina business. He thinks back to the 1973/4 fuel crisis, when cities were in turmoil, cars lined up for gas, nervousness pervaded homes across the country. He visited friends in London.

"Despite these crisis factors, people in London in the winter of 1973/4 were happily going about their business. They had a worse fuel crisis there, much worse than in this country," Hardy notes. "They also had bombings by the IRA and terror tactics that would normally keep people home behind barred doors. Instead, they were going their merry way and the city was thriving."

When he returned after his winter break visiting his old navy buddies, Hardy did some methodical mental calculations. He found his logical legal training handy. No matter what the crisis or the situation, people continue to go about their business after the first shock wears off, he surmised. Careful analysis of the economy as he understood it led him further along his train of thought. He reasoned that when people are under pressure they can do several things. They can flee from the cities to the country, when life in cities becomes intolerable. They must, of course, have the means to flee. Or they can accept the inevitable, become fatalistic, and live for today, to hell with tomorrow, and spend money anyway. Either way, people want to spend money so as to better satisfy their wants and thereby approach their dreams.

He continued his thinking, drawing a pattern across his fertile mind. People continued to achieve happiness, go on vacation, do the things they really wanted to do, despite occasional crisis times, recession or inflation. They bought on time, on credit, mortgaged homes, and spent the money they could get their hands on as they wished.

The facts seemed clear. People intended to spend money. They had desires, needs, demands, wants. Dennis Hardy intended to provide a service and the products that people wanted.

"Lemmings are driven to the sea periodically by natural causes," he observes. "Some signal of nature tells them they must give up their home terrain and hurry off. People can be like lemmings. When something tells them they should have a need satisfied, they want it satisfied."

With the growing amount of leisure time, the increasing expectations that people have today, the seeming endless desire to spend money, Hardy positioned himself solidly in the leisure time field. True, he had the skills to service the working boats of full-time fishermen in his area. They were his bread and butter. He wanted to serve them well. The leisure market was his meat, the fixings, and, eventually, perhaps, also the gravy of his new career.

Time has proved him right. Despite the slow dawning of awareness that there is an energy shortage now and perhaps always will be, people want their needs filled. They still will not be denied their leisure activities. Hardy is there to accommodate them.

Summers are Dennis Hardy's busy season. He works six to seven days a week and overtime nearly every day. He thrives on it. "I can meet a wider cross section of people, good, fun people from every part of the country, from every walk of life right here than anywhere else. They come to me. I work on their boats, their engines, talk with them, listen to them. I see more of life and people than at a sidewalk café in Paris," Hardy says.

His reputation for doing the job right and backing up his work has brought new business to his harborside marina. It isn't fancy. Vacationers might call it picturesque. But the jobs he does stay done. The word gets out. More people come.

"It may seem old fashioned and silly to some, but it really pays to have an old-time philosophy, to do a good job and stand behind it. That pays off more when you are building a business, it pays off much better than the rip-and-run-type job will ever do," he says.

"When people learn they can trust you, they come back and bring their friends. That's good for business. And it's profitable too. Besides," Hardy says as he bends over a quietly purring engine, "There's nothing wrong with making money. If you don't make money, you don't stay in business!"

Learning a mechanic's trade wasn't quick-study work. Hardy spent hours in training. He attended the Evinrude school in Milwaukee and the Outboard Marine Corporation Service schools in Miami and New Jersey, and spent several winters working in giant marinas on the sunny Florida shores. He earned the resounding sum of $4 per hour working with accomplished mechanics. Back in 1971 his services were charged off to boat owners from Chicago and Cleveland and other large northern cities at $12 per hour. Even then, he figured it was good pay. He supplemented it by working thirty more hours a week in a Jewish delicatessen for $2 an hour. The sun was fun and the training was certain to pay off for him in the future, he surmised. He calculated well and correctly.

"You must keep learning. After all the years I spent in formal navy schooling, college and law studies, you might think I would be tired of learning. Actually, you have to keep current all the time. This nuts-and-bolts business takes as much know-how and study as an executive's job, if not more.

"Luckily," he says, "we're still living in a free enterprise system. You can work or play. It's your choice. The incentives are there for anyone who wants to make things happen. The opportunities are better today, probably, than years ago. People have money to spend. If you can provide the service they want, and meet their needs, you're in a position to build a solid, profitable business."

But despite the big decision to forsake the opportunities of a law career and build a small marina, the marina has not become an end in itself.

Several summers ago Dennis Hardy met a pretty young woman at a bank where he did business, and by wintertime they were married. Now Dennis and his wife, Melodie, operate the marina together, sharing in and benefiting from their mutual experiences. Business and off-business time is spent with their one-year-old daughter, Kristen. Dennis now realizes that the material wants and needs of his family have to be satisfied, and that he ultimately is the same consumer he has been serving. At thirty-five, Dennis feels that hard work and the development of realistic options have benefited his life and made it meaningful.

"Maybe someday I'll do something else but right now I'm happy being in the boat repair business, raising a healthy family, and in winter, participating in community activities and projects that make Maine life more meaningful for all."

Who can tell where Dennis's tracks will lead? He's demonstrated that he's introspective enough to know himself, sense his limitations, perceive his abilities, and grasp onto the physical and spiritual elements in life that make him one of the new pioneers.

18/Bob Rouillard— From Banker to Potato Chip Maker

New York's Westchester County, to many people, symbolizes prestige. From that area of hills and fields, country homes and stately manors, Wall Street's bankers and brokers, the advertising, communications, and business executives of Manhattan take the train in to Fun City each day. At night, they board commuter trains to trek back, fleeing from the harsh realities of the work-a-day world to the perfect martini parties of the fabled bedroom communities surrounding the Big Apple.

Other areas also send in their bright, young, bushy-tailed executives. They descend on New York from Greenwich and Stamford, Connecticut, from Montclair, New Jersey and other equally prestigious towns that ring the metropolitan area. Most big cities have these bedroom compounds from which sleepy executives emerge each dawn and to which they sleepily return each evening.

Bob Rouillard was luckier than most. He didn't have to commute. His was a pleasant banker's life amid the Westchester scene. With their five youngsters, Bob and Bonnie Rouillard were involved in many activities in their hometown. They dined, danced, and socialized with a wide group of friends, acquaintances, neighbors, business associates. A banker's life is not just in the bank, deskside, or in executive suites advising customers on financial matters. Bankers must be seen and circulate among the right groups. Banks must build business and gain new accounts regularly. A banker's life doesn't stop when the clock strikes three.

"The job was good and certainly rewarding. We had many close friends in Westchester, too, people we enjoyed and could relax with," Bob recalls. "But things began to change, as all things do, I guess. Bit by bit life didn't seem quite what we thought it should be."

His wife recalls her debutante coming out party and the social whirl of her early life. There were the clubs, Junior League meetings, other activities that kept her busy, along with raising children, managing a home, organizing parties and activities. Many families thrive within these parameters in a frenzied social whirl. Many more strive to reach the levels where they, too, can enjoy the privileges afforded in the right circles within the right towns amid the right people in the right clubs.

"We too were involved in a wide variety of activities. It all seemed perfectly natural for those years," Bob remembers. But bit by bit, the circles became busier. The Rouillards were on a treadmill, like it or not. The circles were moving faster. Business and social life was one round after another of running here, there, and almost everywhere, around and around.

His BA degree from Babson and graduate work at Stoners Graduate School of Banking of Rutgers University provided the credentials a rising bank executive needed. Bob had them, plus a winning smile, brains, and an appropriately imposing appearance. His wife was a Pine Manor girl, schooled in the niceties of life. They were a well-teamed couple, readily climbing the accepted ladder of success in the banking business in their Westchester environment. Without the daily drudgery of commuting to New York, the hours at the National Bank of Westchester didn't seem too long. Home was just a short drive away.

"We lived by the water on Long Island Sound," Bob explains. "But we knew you couldn't use the water unless you belonged to one of the clubs there. Bankers may count lots of money, but they aren't necessarily the best-paid people in town, and clubs do cost money."

As their family grew and their fortunes prospered, the Rouillards began feeling a vague sense of uneasiness that all was not quite as it should be. They continued on the social circuit amid the right people in Westchester County. That was expected of them.

On occasion, they would hear comments at parties about newcomers to the groups. These comments ranged from "Who invited those people," referring to another couple, to "They don't belong here." Bob and Bonnie pondered the comments. They were accepted and acceptable. More than that, they were willing to accept new people if they seemed decent enough. They weren't, however, attuned to or prepared for the rising tide of status-consciousness.

"But, my dear," one matron explained at the close of a party, as she indicated a departing couple to Bob and Bonnie, "these people just aren't the right type. They just aren't 'us'."

"The more we thought about that evening, the more we realized that we were hearing comments like that more frequently," Bob relates. "People, the so-called right people, were becoming more inclined to sneer at those who lived in a smaller house, had an economy car, didn't belong to the best club. We could see a real pecking order developing with harder rules every year. Conformity was being inflicted by the ruling social elite."

Many other areas have the same type of social elite. Many of these elite are, of course, self-appointed. Money seems to breed more snobbery than good manners.

The Rouillards, for business, family, and fun reasons, continued their activities. But they also began thinking more about the comments and actions they observed.

"It seemed that you were judged more and more by the 'right' type of people you knew. You had to join the 'right' club, whether for the beach, golf, boating, whatever," Bob notes. "You had to invite the 'right' people to your parties. You had to be seen at the 'right' places. We were never certain who decided these 'right' parties, invitation lists and activities, but no doubt you were either in the 'in' group or you were out."

Perhaps the social whirl was a symptom of the changing, frantic times in which we all live. Perhaps, also, it is a cause of the escalating frenzy of today's city and suburban life. The Rouillards began to analyze their life and life-style more systematically.

"We began to ask ourselves if this type of life is what we really wanted," Bob explains. "We heard of parties where parents were turning on with their kids. Cocktail parties weren't just social drinking parties: some were becoming drinking events. Some parents seemed to feel they had to get in tune with their kids by smoking pot and drinking with their teenage youngsters."

"Some of the people who were assumed to be the nicest and best parents didn't even know what their children were doing," Bonnie recalls. "The children were actually far down the line in their scale of values. Parties, social acceptability, getting into the right bridge group, golf foursome, tennis circles, was paramount, it seemed. Children were conceived, fed, clothed, steaked and Brooks Brothered, but really ignored as people. We wanted to enjoy our children and give them examples of what we thought were the better things in life. Those better things didn't include, in our minds, constant cocktail parties and status-climbing games. We wanted them to pick friends they liked for who they were, not what they had or how impressive their parents were."

"We realized, the more we thought about the changing social scene, that we believed in simpler, basic values," Bob notes.

Bonnie had a knack for stitchery. She had often wanted to open a little shop where she and friends could display their sewing skills and have the fun and profit of their own creations.

"You don't do that in Westchester County, where we lived," she observes. "Nice people don't own shops and go to work in them. I really didn't feel that as a banker's wife in the environment of that particular area, I could open a shop. Bankers' wives don't do that." Actually, looking back, she probably could and should have pursued her ambition to have a place of her own if that was what she wanted. But in their circle, abiding by the rules of suburbia that they saw, a shop was not appropriate.

The more they discussed the idea of starting over, the more the idea made sense. They wanted to hold on to their personal values, to raise their family as a family and enjoy what they perceived as basic values together.

Other things began to bug Bob and Bonnie. The numbers game was one. Titles were another.

"People among the elite seemed to keep track of your achievements by your title. They knew which desk you occupied and what level that meant you had achieved in their business hierarchy. They knew and actually seemed intent on finding out which number parking spot you had. That was clear evidence of how you ranked in your career at the bank, the office, the business."

Bob began his search for what he wanted, a life and life-style that would permit him and his family to return to their basic values. His search by car, plane, and train took him to many towns. He answered ads for bankers in southern, mid-Atlantic, and northern parts of the country.

He was offered positions in other areas. Some had excellent financial promise, but they offered more of the same social whirl. He remembers amazing himself when he first uttered the silly-sounding phrase, "Money isn't everything." But he did and does believe that.

Comparing notes with Bonnie and their children, Bob remembers vividly their final decision to move to Maine. There was a good position available at one of the leading banks. His background fit perfectly. More important, he recalls, he liked the people, the low-key approach of native Mainers and the "away" people who had moved to the state.

"They had a different approach to life. It was more realistic and down to earth," Bob points out. "People respect workers in Maine. They look up to a person who is on his own, in business, who works to accomplish something. That sold me," he adds.

Pulling up roots from the affluence of suburban Westchester was not exactly traumatic, but it did involve some wrenching moments. The Rouillards had been to Maine, but didn't know that much about living there full time. They reasoned they should be prepared.

"All of us decided to update our physicals, have dental work done before we moved," Bonnie recalls. "I spent three months at the dentist's office, having root canal work completed. It seemed logical to have it done in 'civilization,' because we had no idea whether there were any dentists in the north woods. Our friends in Westchester had us about convinced that we were moving to the last frontier of primeval forest, perhaps even Arctic desolation, where doctors visited on horseback. Now that we know better, we haven't told them differently."

What the Rouillards found was far different from what their suburban contemporaries anticipated. They discovered quickly that the natives aren't restless. Fact is, they found a warmth and openness that surprised them. They discovered that their new neighbors were quick to welcome them, help them settle in, provide advice on doctors, dentists, plumbers, electricians, and anything else they needed, including where to find reliable auto repair people.

"We still laugh about our first fears," Bonnie says. "We had bought a three-year supply of medication on the assumption that we were going on safari. Friends in Westchester actually warned us that we'd come running back there the first time we were snowbound."

For several years, Bob was content in the banking world of Maine. He became deeply involved in working with business people, helping them improve their operations, advising them on better use of working capital, how to improve cash flow, devising marketing methods to build larger sales and expand distribution.

"I enjoyed it," Bob says emphatically. "Many were turnaround situations. People would come in for a business loan but their profit-and-loss statements were terrible. First, we had to help them reorganize so we could lend them money. Then, I'd spend sometimes days and weeks helping them use the loans to make more money so we would be repaid on time.

"Many of these people were anxious for business advice and help. They apreciated my efforts and that's a real pleasure, to work with men and women who know how to say thanks. Bankers don't get that very often.

"They have a solid, old-fashioned work ethic and want to be successful. That made my job easier."

During his several years with Canal Bank, Bob traveled a large part of southern Maine. He functioned in many capacities beyond that of a mere loan officer. In effect, he was a business doctor, diagnosing problem areas, prescribing solutions to make the business healthy, productive, and profitable. The more he saw of business opportunities, the more he realized he had a desire to get directly involved in a business of his own. So, he did.

"One older businessman had a sound operation, but its potential was much greater than he wanted. He was happy with a good, steady operation, but was looking ahead to retirement from his daily workload," Bob explains. "A friend I had met had a strong background in the areas in which I needed strength: sales and distribution. I had the banking, accounting, and other business background. We thought and worked well together," Bob adds, "so we bought Circus Time Potato Chips."

Potatoes are famous in Maine. And potato chips and other snack foods are a booming nationwide industry.

"I may not have had any particular expertise in the potato chip and snack food business," Bob says with a grin, "but I sure have eaten enough of them at ball games."

Bob had met his Circus Time partner, Bill Leonardi, during his banking days. They teamed up, buckled down, and began their new potato chipping careers. There's more to the business than slicing, cooking, and bagging, they discovered.

"Fortunately, Bill is a super salesman. He's great with customers and happens to have another natural asset besides his wit and smile. He's mechanically inclined. He never had technical training, he's just one of those people who can take something apart and put it back together so it works better than before. He's been doing it since he was eight or nine years old," Bob adds.

That ability, he explains, enabled them to streamline their packing operation and make repairs as fast as needed, rather than waiting a week for a service representative to show up.

Bob's strengths, gained from his experience as a business doctor, also were put to the test. He knew how to organize purchasing, how to work with capital, obtain SBA loans, plan repayment schedules, shop for short- and long-term financing.

"I always told business people that they should have a good accountant and a good banker if they wanted to really prosper. And I had emphasized the simple fact that they should take their banker into their confidence and talk with him, get his advice, use all the bank's considerable services as necessary before any problems arose. That's the best way to avoid money problems and business ones—preventive management rather than emergency treatment when you are in trouble," Bob states.

There were times that Rouillard had second thoughts and even strong misgivings. Taking your own advice is more difficult than you may believe.

"I would sometimes ask myself, can I really do this, can I make it go the way it should?" Bob remembers vividly. "When you work as an executive for a large company, you have a large staff of specialists at your command. All of a sudden, in a small business, there's just you. You're responsible for sixty-plus employees, their families, their children, and your own family too. Every decision that must be made is your own. Whatever happens, you are responsible. That can get hairy." Bob grins wryly.

"You have to be a purchasing agent, a shipping agent, an accountant, a bookkeeper. You must coordinate your supplies so they arrive on time at one end of the plant and have the bags, boxes, paper, tape, stickers, all the supplies to pack the product at the other end of the processing line. One shipment off, and you shut down the line and send everybody home for the day. We haven't had to do it, but we've come close at times when a truckload of supplies was missing during blizzard weather," he explains.

"Getting into a business overnight is like having quints," Bob points out. "It's much easier to raise one child at a time or do one job at a time. When you are responsible for twenty different jobs each day, you sometimes meet yourself coming around the corner."

"Being in business for myself rather than helping others in business was more of a shock than I had expected," Bob says. Bonnie agrees that at times he had a somewhat dazed expression after fourteen hours at the Circus Time plant.

"We had to decide to buy oil at a price. Maybe it would

go up, maybe down. Which is the right time to stock up? We had to design new bags. Which design would have the greatest sales appeal at the point of purchase? We needed more trucks—which would be the most efficient, economical, reliable, when every salesperson says his is the truck just right for us? There are decisions every day. Suggesting ideas to someone else is easy compared to making that final decision yourself . . . and then spending your money on it. You're betting on yourself several days every week."

Rouillard feels it took him nearly a year to appreciate the total picture of his business. There were no committees, no key staff people to delegate assignments to, no one with a dry shoulder to cry on when things went bad. There was no board, no directors, no managers, nobody but Bob and Bill and, fortunately, dedicated, hard-working employees, plus the former owner. Bob and his partner had asked the owner to stay on until they felt comfortable with the business.

"He had purposely held growth back a bit so he could handle the business himself. He was conservative in business. If business grew so big that he couldn't oversee it personally, he didn't want that growth." This conservative, frugal, Yankee business-mindedness proved an asset. Bob and Bill wanted growth. They agree they may have moved ahead too fast and perhaps in the wrong directions. The former owner served as both a sounding board and a brake on their tendency toward excessive forward momentum.

From the thirty-five trucks they inherited with the business, they built a fleet of forty-five and added several more later. Through Bill's sales efforts, they expanded into new areas and gained stronger market penetration in areas they already served. Their business isn't confined to potato chips, as the company name implies. They pop and sell bagged popcorn. They have a variety of other snack food products, too, from pickled eggs to lamb's tongues in jars. They also provide, with their expanded fleet of trucks, distribution for products of other firms that need sales delivery in the New England states.

Presently, their lines are sold in Maine and much of New Hampshire. They split up sales territories for greater market penetration. The key to greater volume is not just big supermarkets but also the smaller stores, the convenience stores, tourist spots, and everywhere that hungry people shop.

Rouillard and Leonardi added other items, too, from pretzels to cheese snacks. They began private label manufacturing, producing products and packaging under a customer's desired brand name. They've tested new flavors for chips and snacks from cheese to barbecue tastes.

"Adding new lines is important to sales growth, of course," Bob points out. "When your trucks are delivering several items, they can also deliver other products on the same trip. Multiple product sales add nicely to the profit picture.

"Dropping some items is just as important, but many people tend to overlook that fact," he adds. "It pays to check your sales figures and product popularity periodically. Perhaps you can boost sales with advertising or new packaging, maybe contests and special pricing to your customers. At times, some items just don't earn their keep. It's best to drop them and concentrate on those that are making a profit. That's where cost accounting comes in handy. And," he grins, "a good accountant to help you analyze the figures. Sometimes you get so close to or fond of a product yourself that you don't realize it may not really be worth continuing. Giant food firms do this. They regularly drop unprofitable lines. Smaller ones like ours must too, if we want to keep that bottom line profitable."

With children in college, Bob also thought about selling the school and college market. The previous owner hadn't tapped that sales field. Bob and Bill did and are expanding in it, feeding the voracious appetites of students throughout their trade area.

Working twelve to fourteen hours a day, Bob Rouillard has been happy. But he also began listening to his wife, whom he seldom saw since buying his own business.

"We were having fun enough. The challenge was exciting and business was great, but making money wasn't why we had left Westchester," Bonnie points out. Bob agrees, "We really wanted more time with the children, to watch them grow up, to help them in sports." The Rouillard boys are hockey nuts. They also are involved in soccer and other sports.

With business prospering, chips chipping, pretzel sales snapping, and profits rising, Bob and Bonnie took another hard look at their life, their goals, their life-style. And they changed gears again.

"You should reexamine yourself, your goals or objectives and what makes you really tick every now and then," Bob believes.

"We had begun to overlook what we came to Maine for," Bonnie says. Bob endorses that.

"We hadn't taken a family vacation for years. I had missed hockey and soccer games. I often didn't get to see the kids for days at a time. So, we went back to basics again," Bob explains. "Watching our sons, and having become involved with their hockey club, I decided this was important, so I helped organize the Youth Hockey Association."

Bob sold his interest in Circus Time. The depth of experience he gained in the two years running it, he now applies to another business miles nearer home.

"Money isn't everything," he still believes. "Time is much more important." He is more emphatic about that point now.

Today, he is a partner in a meat wholesaling business, based in a neighboring town. That owner wanted time to do other things himself, like concentrate on his hotel and restaurant. Timing was right for both.

"Fact is," Rouillard is quick to emphasize, "timing is

vital to much of business. You can work your whole life for someone else, or yourself, and not get things to really click if your timing is off. Or," he adds, "if you can't spot opportunities and take advantage of them when the time is right. That skill comes with experience, plus a fair amount of gut instinct."

This time around, Bob intends to take a slower path in growth and business expansion. He intends to have more time for his family and the things they can do together.

"Too many people in business want to grow for growth's sake itself. They think expansion is a constant necessity. But when you push for growth, you must expand your building, add more trucks, hire more people. That adds to overhead, fixed overhead. That means you must keep growing to cover that and make a profit. So you plunge headlong after more growth, you get big and bigger.

"You can put yourself on your own treadmill or in a hospital bed that way."

Rouillard plans to keep tight reins on his inner urge to grow too fast. A tidy profit and the time to enjoy life holds higher priority with him now, he's certain.

"In this respect, I guess I'm becoming more like many people here in Maine and New England. With this beautiful countryside, mountains for skiing, lakes and rivers for fishing, boating, swimming, and sports opportunities and family fun things to do, why rush life?" he reasons. He's in good company. Many other new pioneers feel the same.

Bonnie, too, has changed her life-style. Still an avid mother who follows each youngster's sports and school activities to the minute, she has finally opened her own business, called, appropriately, Port Stitchery. In a rustic building with panoramic views of the port and river, she cheerfully welcomes customers each day. Through her creative hands, the attractive crafts flow together. From her shop they flow into tourist cars to decorate homes along the Atlantic coast. She teaches, too, helping others relearn the art of needlepoint and other fine stitchery she adores.

Watching Bonnie lead a needlepoint group, while Bob figures his accounts at the kitchen table, warmed by a wood-burning stove, one sees a far different couple from the one in Westchester. They not only are, but look the part of, new pioneers.

19/Judith Hansen— From Teacher to Newspaper Reporter

Raised on a farm in the backwoods of Maine, Judith Hansen never expected to become the talented, bylined, reporter-photographer she is today. Part of her success can no doubt be measured by her dawning awareness (almost phase-by-phase in her life) that a woman can and should pursue her own personal goals.

Looking back, Judith has analyzed many of the factors that eventually focused her concentration, and more importantly, her determination, on a fulfilling career.

"My father packed us off to this lovely farm in the boonies and took off to sea when I was young," she recalls. She grew up in a town that had one store, one gas station, a post office, and an active 4-H club. She attended school, participated in 4-H club activities considered appropriate for girls growing up on a farm, drank lots of raw milk, and churned homemade butter.

"Tradition was deeply rooted in that area," Judith explains. "If you were a girl, tradition dictated that you learn to cook, raise and preserve vegetables, sew and do all the other things that would train you to be a wife and mother. People didn't ask then, and still may not today, in that type of area, what you wanted to be yourself. They ask how many children you plan to have and when you plan to settle down to raise a family.

"Boys went to college to study for a career, but girls weren't supposed to think of a career other than a family, except," she adds, "if you wanted to be a nurse, a teacher, or an airline stewardess."

When she tried discussing the future with friends, they seemed puzzled by her questions. It was assumed that girls didn't aspire to careers. Even the discussions with high school guidance advisors didn't offer many challenging options.

"We took aptitude tests," she reflects, "and those test scores were supposed to tell you what you might be good at, but the guidance counseling then didn't focus on helping you select a career for yourself. Actually, I didn't know what I wanted to do and there were really no people who could give me a range of options or explore career potentials for a woman."

Fortunately, as she looks back, her family was open-minded and not bound by the traditions that seemed to hold others captive in her hometown. Judith was encouraged to think critically, to explore ideas and not fall into a pattern. She credits this open attitude and supportive wisdom of her mother with preventing her from becoming pigeon-holed in a housewife/mother role. To expand her horizons, although she had not yet set career objectives, Judith headed to college.

"I changed majors six times and in the process wrote a lot of term papers, did reports, and generally found that I didn't have a clear idea of what I wanted to do or be."

Her career prospecting progressed into teaching,

which she found both challenging and exhilarating, but somewhat awesome.

"It is exciting, helping to mold young people, helping them focus on their potential and abilities so they can learn more about themselves and their world," she believes. As she taught, she also met her future (and former) husband.

"He had a sense of humor. He talked and listened, and we were comfortable socially. He wasn't boring." While he was in the service she continued teaching in Virginia but her quandary remained: whether to get married or not. She didn't want to get married, but she didn't want to give him up either, she remembers. Eventually, she returned to New England and a new, more challenging job, teaching in the Roxbury area of Boston. It was an area known for its turmoil in the schools and, often, in the streets.

When her future husband returned from military service in 1968, they dated again and were married in 1969. That, she feels, was another phase that focused her in the direction she finally took. While her husband continued his education to become an accountant, Judith continued to teach.

"For some reason, I was terrified of the middle America syndrome, of becoming like so many others who settled into a suburban rut," she explains.

The next few years were busy, working to support them both while he finished graduate school. In the process, they socialized with other couples who were headed into the routine of the traditional business world.

"Suburban syndrome" still haunted her as her husband became an accountant and entered the whirl of the business world in which he expected to achieve financial success.

"I wasn't the type, I guess, who could be satisfied with convention for convention's sake," Judith points out. "Talk at social events centered on families and children and business."

It was not, she realized, the world she had anticipated

or even wanted. She decided that since these social events held little interest, she would avoid them, and she stopped going to the usual, accepted round of business-social parties.

As she sought her own dimensions, Judith took a year off to think about the future and what it held for her. More importantly, she thought of what she really wanted to achieve, to do, to be. She still refers to this period as her "time of thinking." She wrote down her strengths and weaknesses as she saw them. She tried to chart on paper and in her mind the direction she felt she must take.

During her year of thinking, her mother was supportive, as was her husband. Even with that support, the decision to follow her insights and pursue a personally fulfilling life was hers alone to make.

"The more I thought about myself and what I should do, the more I realized that I never really wanted to settle down," she explains. "You only go around once, so why not explore what you really want and can achieve. If you don't strive to be everything you can, to explore every aspect of yourself, you may find yourself looking back when you are sixty or seventy and wondering whether you could have done other things, really worthwhile things. I didn't want to reach that point and look back and realize I had never tried.

"This may sound self-centered, but it isn't," she points out. "But I felt and still do feel that if you can give more to other people you can be more yourself. If you develop your energies and abilities you can give more to others and receive more from them."

Judith Hansen began exploring other dimensions of herself. She probed her likes and dislikes, her motives and abilities, strengths and failings. She also applied for and got a part-time public relations position in Boston. That experience was her turning point as a new pioneer. She elected to stay in Boston while her husband switched jobs and moved to a nearby state to further his career. Her supervisor was a woman who was able to challenge and teach, advise and prod, to bring out the best in coworkers.

"I realized while working there that I didn't have another woman as a friend, until then," Judith says. "Women often have this problem. They make friends of the wives of their husband's friends. We women have poor self-images. In fact, while I was married I seemed to have lived through an era of a derived identity."

Meeting the new challenges of writing and handling public relations assignments, Judith now faced her highest hurdle on the road to starting over.

She saw three options for the future. She could continue in public relations, she could turn to journalism and reporting full-time, which attracted her strongly, or she could join her husband. That, she recalls, was a key turning point.

While considering her options, Judith had attended courses in photography and journalism. She found the field fascinating. In the process, on the job and at classes, she had met other women who already had undergone similar periods of questioning. They became friends, discussed their views on career potentials and options for personally satisfying lives. From this mutual understanding grew mutual respect. As that grew, so did Judith's self-esteem.

Her personal family fireworks flared on the Fourth of July, she recalls. She had decided to pursue a writing career. Her husband argued against continued pursuit of a separate career. Rockets went off.

"It was over that day," she points out. "And the next day I had already accepted an interview for a job. I won't ever forget that July Fourth."

As she recalls, "Actually, about a month before the final flareup, I had thought that I might be single again. I tried to honestly think about where I wanted to live, what I wanted to do. I realized I wanted to be free to think for myself, to meet people, to follow more exciting challenges rather than settle into suburban life."

She interviewed for a newspaper job in a coastal New England town. Before the interview began, she sorted out her personal priorities. She wanted a place to live where she could be happy, free, and independent. She wanted a job that satisfied her intellectually. And she wanted to face a challenge each day and win. Money was important to live, but, she believes, money was far down on her priority list.

Judith experienced the typical buffeting that comes during a divorce. It puzzled her at the time, but she had become more philosophical about that period of her first faltering steps as a new pioneer.

"Friends are the people who help you back up when you're really down," she explains. "Some married people think a divorce is contagious. You may have been 'good friends' for years. They visited your house and you and your husband visited their home. But when they hear about your divorce, they seem to think you're on the make, a threat to their nest. Friends who were sweet little lovebirds turn into avenging eagles. Their talons are aimed right at your throat."

Judith has started over, enthusiastically and eagerly. The trying decisions are behind her now.

"Interviewing for a newspaper job, or I guess any job, is difficult when you're on your own. There was a time, while I was with my husband, when I felt protected, loved, shielded, even in my independence. Now, on my back porch, with friends around to talk about ideas and think what we want to think, I feel protected by my freedom and independence," she says.

Reporting, she feels, suits her personality. She began with a community beat and ranged from local news to human interest features, which she uncovered on her reporting rounds.

"No two days are alike. I'm meeting many people, all different and with their individual stories to tell. Reporting is like exploring parts of the world," Judith says with apparent enthusiasm. "I can explore their world, and as I do my job, I am expanding my own world too."

Blessed or cursed, depending on your viewpoint, Judith has an insatiable curiosity. That, she believes, is what makes her especially good in her new career, the one she finally found.

"Writing is exploring in a way, discussing things about people and what they do and identifying with their experiences," Judith says, emphatically. "Often I realize that a part of what they are saying is something I've experienced. That helps me to understand and interpret their experiences so I can tell their story better, more effectively, when I put it on paper."

In her new career she finds herself surrounded by creative, talented, dedicated people. The local newspaper in many ways is like hundreds of other papers, with lively reporters scrambling after the news each week. Perhaps more importantly, it has become a unique newspaper, with literally hundreds of awards won by staff members, editors, and the paper itself. The long-time owner and publisher, Alexander Brook, was himself a new pioneer twenty years ago. He left the import-export field and New York for the challenge of a weekly paper. During those twenty years he assembled a highly talented team of creative, free-thinking new pioneers and brought the paper to national prominence as an often-honored weekly, the *York County Coast Star*.

Today, Judith Hansen works as part of that team, enriched by the stimulating abilities of other reporters and continually challenged by them and her own inner drive.

"I'm surrounded in the community and on the job with intellectually stimulating, fun people. Every day, every assignment is different. In this type of work you can be free thinking, keep an open mind to analyze and develop the important aspects of the stories. People are interested in other people, in the human side of them as well as what they do. As you write a news item or a feature story in depth, you must rely on your own instincts and mental judgments. It's hard work. There have been many weeks when I've spent sixty hours on the job," Judith points out.

Her initial stories about local events led to others. Her byline on articles and under the photographs she takes covering her subjects, have won her deserved recognition. With her personal sensitivity and feeling for the people she interviews, her features reveal her growing capabilities as a writer.

"Other reporters and writers feel the same way," she maintains. "Putting a story together, digging out the bits and pieces and seeing the story come together on your typewriter is like giving birth. Sometimes the story seems to write itself, especially when you can reflect the human elements of the people you have interviewed."

For her, she realizes, reporting and writing are more than work. They are her job, true enough, but they are her recreation as well. The stimulation of meeting dozens of new people every week, cementing friendships with those she has met and worked with before, carries her to a crest of exhilaration.

Her insatiable curiosity leads her happily into the next week and month, seeking new stories that will fill more pages. Time is immaterial to her as she pursues the new life-style and career she has begun and is building for herself.

"Probably the most important aspect of my new life is the fact that people judge you for what you are and do, not what you have."

Home is now a comfortable house on Turbots Creek. Home is also her job and her community of people in the York County area of coastal Maine.

Judith Hansen has started over, with enthusiasm and new zest for life. She is well along the trail of the new pioneers, living her life and being part of the lives of others she so accurately reflects in her reporting.